Finding a Way
stories from a creative life

Bar Scott

ALM
BOOKS

2020

*An audio version of
Finding a Way,
narrated by Bar Scott,
is available at Audible and other outlets.*

© 2020 Bar Scott
Please feel free to share these stories with someone you love.

Published by Bar Scott/ALM Books
961 SW Washington Avenue
Corvallis, Oregon
www.barscott.com

Cover Layout, Erin Papa at The Turning Mill, Palenville, NY
Book Layout © 2017 BookDesignTemplates.com
Cover and interior photographs, ©2020 Bar Scott
Author Photograph ©2014 Franco Vogt
(add six years to my face to know what I look like now)

Inspiration, Memoir, Self-Help/Creativity

Finding a Way/ Bar Scott. -- 1st ed.
ISBN 9798623454140

Do what you love and success will follow.

*I thought that meant cash, visibility,
and better odds that my calls would be returned.
Writing these stories reminded me that when you
do what you love, what you get is a meaningful life.*

Contents

To hear the songs described in this book, scan this code

or visit barscott.com/book-songs

Simple Gifts 1

Catching My Breath 11

The Ways of Water 29

Singing With Others 43

Before and After 51

Grapes and Seeds 61

Willy and Me 69

My Old Man 75

Here and There 81

Birthday 89

Out of the Blue 95

Anatomy of a Song 101

Blinded 107

Breaking Bread 119

Valentine 133

A Little Love 137

A Conversation 143

Filled up 147

A Good Long Drink 155

This Lane is My Lane 169

Gratitude 176

• Beginning •

Simple Gifts

I was twenty-eight when I bought a small house next to West Laurel Hill Cemetery outside Philadelphia. It was 1986. My grandparents had been buried there a couple of years earlier, so every so often I'd walk to their spot and say hello. Their son William was buried there too. He died when he was two from complications of spina bifida. There's only one stone for the three of them. William's name is carved on the side. You wouldn't see it unless you knew to look. I like that they're all there together. It tells me something about the longevity of love. My mother was born shortly before William died so probably only remembers the absence of him.

While I was living in that house, I bought a two-and-a-half octave Casio keyboard to see if I could sing and play at the same time. It was small enough that I could carry it around. One summer afternoon I took it up to my bedroom and lay down with it in my lap. I cycled through the sounds it could make to see if any of them would inspire me to sing along. I was just starting to write songs back then. Like most keyboards my Casio had a synthesized vocal patch that sounded like a hundred voices singing in unison. With the push of a key a choir would sing Ah for as many seconds as you were willing to hold it down. A low D-flat sounded good to me that afternoon so I held it and started to sing. In high school I sang in the school and church choirs. Those were medium-sized—25 to 30 people. Senior year I joined the regional choir. There were 200 of us in that one. I was an alto. With all those voices singing together we produced a lot of sound. But it was the silence between phrases that moved me. They were like waves at the beach. You knew they were coming but there was a hush while you waited. And sometimes we sang so quietly I felt like my body might lift away from my feet.

During one of our concerts, I sang a solo on the spiritual "Deep River" while the rest of the choir hummed quietly behind me. Deep River/My home is over Jordan/Deep River/I want to cross over into campground. I didn't understand the lyrics then, but I could feel them moving through me like a message. Standing in front of an audience with a choir of singers behind me was both exhilarating and humbling. The sound of sustained human voices in harmony is one that has always moved me, but that night was the first time I was aware of it.

So when I turned my Casio on and played a D-flat for what must have been twenty minutes, it was natural for me to sing something that sounded like a hymn. Grace is the song that came out of that bedroom experiment. It has only one line of lyrics: Thank the world for giving me all the reasons that I have to sing. The rest of the melody is vocalized on various vowel sounds depending on my mood when I sing it. The first time I sang it for anyone else was for my extended family. I asked my father in advance if I could say grace at our upcoming

Thanksgiving dinner. Saying grace had always been his job, but he was glad to have me do it. Looking back, asking for this change was a testament to my need to be heard.

When I stood up to sing, twenty-seven members of my family were looking back at me, sitting at uneven tables pushed together and covered with white tablecloths. I was scared. These were the people I loved more than anything in the world. There was a lot to lose. What if they didn't like my song or they were uncomfortable with the time it took to sing it? What if I sang out of tune or I lost my place? But when I started to sing, they bowed their heads and listened.

I've sung Grace in some remarkable places since that night. On New Year's Eve in 2005, I sang it at the Annual Peace Concert in the Cathedral Church of St John the Divine in New York, the largest gothic cathedral in North America. The place was packed with over 3000 people. The spotlights were bright, and the space was so big I couldn't see faces beyond the third row. There was no reason to be afraid. The lyrics were easy to remember, and the melody was mine to improvise. I was more excited than scared. I stood in the center of the sacristy as the organist began to play a low D-flat on the pipe organ behind me. The entire space filled with the pulse of that one note. I'd learned during my sound check that whatever I sang lingered in the room for a long time—eight seconds the sound engineer said. Because of that, I sang my lines slowly and waited for each phrase to disappear before I sang the next one. Controlling the time like that was thrilling: the silence between phrases, the harmonics that lingered and bounced off the masonry walls. It was as beautiful a sound as I'd ever heard. It was hard to believe it was coming from me. Yet somehow I knew there was more to it than that.

In late February 2002 I got a call from a filmmaker named Rick who had heard me sing at a concert in Upper Black Eddy, Pennsylvania a few years earlier. Shafts of light from a full moon streamed through the skylights in our living room. I was leaning against the wall, the phone propped against my ear, looking out into the night. After he introduced himself, he said, "I'm doing a film on the healing power of music. I'd like you to be a part of it." As he described his project, my eyes filled with tears, my heart felt bigger in my chest. I couldn't respond. It was as though this man I didn't know was rescuing me. My son Forrest had died two weeks earlier. He was three-and-a-half. He'd been diagnosed with liver cancer when he was two. I was still in shock. Rick Korn was giving me a reason to live, something to look forward to, a purpose.

Two months later when his film was finished, Rick introduced me to Lisa Luckett who had lost her husband on 9-11. She was planning a concert at the Beacon Theater in New York City to thank the 2500 first responders who had tried to find her husband in the rubble. Phoebe Snow, Beth Nielsen-Chapman, Delores Holmes, and I were asked to headline that event. I'd listened to Phoebe's "Poetry Man" in tenth grade as much as I'd listened to Tapestry a few years earlier. I knew every inflection in Phoebe's voice. I'd heard of Beth but didn't know her music. She'd written a few hits for Nashville singers. And Delores had started her career with Bruce Springsteen in Asbury Park. Her sisters would be singing with us too. Despite the circumstances, I could hardly wait.

A week before the concert, we were all invited to Ground Zero. Escort vehicles and Port Authority

Personnel who had worked in the pit for months met us at the upper gates. The clean-up had just ended. It was July 2002. The sun was bright and beginning to set. We climbed into police vehicles and drove down into the deep, gray earth.

The trip was slow and reverent. So many lives had been lost there. At the bottom, one of the policemen told us to wander around to get a feel for the place. He wanted us to understand what they'd felt like down there.

We took off one by one. It was a time for solitude and reflection. The ground was uneven and hard. I was aware that I was walking on bedrock. The 65-foot concrete walls that had supported the towers were covered with rusty cuts and scrapes. The empty subway tunnels looked like giant conduits that emptied into the vast concrete pool we were standing in. I felt like I'd drown if someone turned the water on. Stairwells led nowhere. A fine, dust from pulverized computers, phones, light fixtures, and everything else that had died there covered the vacant space. It was silent even though the streets above us were alive with energy.

When our group gathered again forty-five

minutes later, we faced each other in a circle in the middle of that emptiness. We shared our thoughts and asked a few questions. Then Rick asked if I would sing Grace. I was glad he asked. Singing was the perfect antidote for what I was feeling.

After a moment I took the deepest breath I could manage and started to hum. I looked at Delores and her sisters and encouraged them to join me. When I started the melody, I thought of Forrest and smiled. I looked up at the sky. I thought about the day the towers fell and all that had happened since. I could feel tears running down my cheeks. Yet there I was. Singing. How had this happened? How could it be that I was singing in this incredible place? Or that my song created with a Casio keyboard on a summer afternoon fifteen years earlier would be a comfort to people who had been through so much?

When the concert at The Beacon started the following week, the lights went down and the show began with a short film. The opening scene was of me singing Grace in the pit. I hadn't realized I was being filmed. I saw myself look up at the sky. I remembered thinking about Forrest. I saw black mascara running down my face. Then I saw the Port

Authority police who had gone down into the pit with us. Their faces were wet too. These were men who might not have been willing to cry in public before 9-11. I call that grace.

Grace

Thank the world for giving me
 all the reasons that I have to sing

Scan this code to hear Grace, or visit barscott.com/book-songs

• Longing •

Catching My Breath

The building was abandoned as far as I could see. A rusty hoist that hadn't been used in decades loomed high above a crumbling loading dock. Metal stairs closed in with moldy corrugated plastic hung from the side of the building and vines swallowed up the chain link fence that once kept trespassers out. I was at the right address but it sure didn't feel right. The only car in the lot was a beat-up bronze van.

I parked my mom's silver Cutlass Supreme next to the van, checked my face in the mirror, and got out. The old mill hidden on a back road to the Schuylkill River must have thrived at one time, but now the water below it was shallow and still. The flesh under my arms was sticky.

As I walked towards the loading dock my nerves were on high alert. I'd never been anywhere near a place like this. There was a sign on the wall with an arrow pointing up. The stairs were sturdy, but I didn't feel safe. At the top there was a solid metal door and a doorbell. A handwritten 3x5 card said *Wait for the Buzzer*. I pushed the white button and a long metallic sound came out of nowhere. When nothing more happened, I hit the bell again. Then I heard feet shuffling towards me from inside. I was tempted to run back down the stairs and drive away but something stronger kept me there.

The door swung towards me. A man with dark brown, wavy hair and a bright green hoodie said, "You must be Bar."

"Sorry about that," I said as I tried to slow my heart down. "I didn't understand the buzzer."

"I figured," he said. "It happens all the time. It's security. You're meant to pull the door open when you hear that sound." It was the first of many things I would learn that day. "I'm Joe by the way."

My heart was still beating hard, but I faked my

way through that first conversation. "I've lived a couple miles from here my whole life, but I've never seen this place before."

"Yeah, I know. It's off the beaten track, that's for sure. Come on in."

He followed me down a short corridor to a sitting area. It looked comfortable—the kind of place where you could put your feet up. The furniture was rough, as though it had been handed down a few times. The rug was worn. I was beginning to relax, but I still wasn't sure. No one knew where I was, and I couldn't shake the idea that I was alone in a collapsing building with a man I didn't know.

"Why don't we start here," Joe said, pointing to a solid door covered with bits of rug. There were three steps up but no banister. "Go 'head. You go first."

I tried the door, but it was tight in its frame. I wasn't sure how hard to push, and I didn't want to break anything.

"Here," he said, "let me help. It's heavy so we can keep the noise out."

He pushed from behind me and the door gave way.

Inside, the room was glowing. Breathing almost.

The overhead lights were dimmed and hundreds of tiny green, red, and blue lights were blinking and not-blinking. This was a room I could not have imagined but was way more than I might have imagined if I'd known how.

On the far wall behind sliding glass doors, two stainless steel 24-track recording machines were backlit and glowing. 12-inch reels of analog tape were threaded in place. Beside them, two six-foot racks of outboard gear, stood at attention, ready for whatever came next. To my right, on a raised floor, were two brown leather couches, and to my left, the hub of it all: a six-foot long, three-foot-wide, 48-channel recording console. Three sets of speakers were perched to its left and right, and a plate glass window in front of it looked out over a bigger space beyond. I was in the right place after all. This was the control room of Kajem Recording Studio.

Not long ago, my mother sent a big brown envelope filled with my childhood homework assignments. My second-grade teacher must have asked us to write about what we wanted to be when we grew up. I wrote, *I want to be a teen-aged beatle because everybody in my family likes the Beatles. My sister has a picture of them.*

I'd seen the Beatles' debut on The Ed Sullivan Show two years earlier. Paul tossed his hair around on "I Want to Hold Your Hand" and screamed with abandon on "I Saw Her Standing There." He looked as surprised as anyone to realize tossing his hair was all it took to drive a nation of women and girls crazy.

My homework assignment included a crayon drawing of The Beatles debut on Ed Sullivan. Ringo and his drums are on a riser behind Paul, George, and John holding their instruments, all of them in black suits, white shirts, black ties, and bowls of solid black crayon hair. I put three-quarter-inch dots in purple, red, and yellow all over the page to represent the lights on stage. I hadn't noticed yet, that Paul was left-handed.

The picture of the Beatles my sister had was a life-sized color poster my father bought and tacked on the wall next to the dartboard in the basement. I thought their pointy black boots and their straight brown pants were the ultimate in cool. And I loved the way they goofed around. They reminded me of how me and my four sisters and my brother goofed around, scrunching up our faces to look like blowfish, and bopping each other on the head like the Three Stooges.

Paul was my favorite then. He smiled all the time and sang as though he was the luckiest guy in the world. After Sgt. Pepper, though, I switched to John. He was intense and dark. I fell for that in the same way I fell for Joyce, Faulkner, and a guy named Brian who rolled his own cigarettes when I got to college. Later, when the Beatles were history and they all started making solo albums, I switched to George. I wanted to be as peaceful and calm as he looked.

But Ringo was always special. I'm a sucker for underdogs, but it was more than that. Until a few months ago when a friend of mine told me I was wrong, I thought he'd sung lead on "You Know My Name (Look Up the Number)", the B-Side of "Let it Be." I played it endlessly—memorized every bit of it including the lounge singer affectations midway through the song. I even made my Aunt Nina listen to all 4 minutes and 19 seconds of it over the phone. I put the receiver up to the speaker on my record player. She listened to the whole thing and said well that was fun when the song was over. How could I not love her? But of course John sang it.

I still have the 45 of that song. It's in a blue and white psychedelic box with a carrier handle on the top at the back of my closet. The entire Scott family collection of 45s is in that box: "Working in a Coal Mine," "Michael the Lover," "The Sound of Silence" and maybe 50 more. I lucked out. All the 45s and Beatles' LPs our family listened to fell into my hands. They're scratched and moldy and I never listen to them, but I love them anyway.

The Black and White TV at our house was a big piece of furniture in the dining room. I remember the night The Jackson Five debuted on Ed Sullivan almost six years after the Beatles. I was eleven. Michael was a month older than me. Our television was so big that standing up my eyes were at the same level as his. The TV itself was still a bit of a miracle but watching Michael—seeing him dance and hearing his voice—was an even bigger one. I was mesmerized. I watched with my fingers in my mouth and my eyes fixed on him. He sang "I Want You Back" and thrilled the world. It looked like the most fun a kid could have.

The first live concert I went to was a whole different thing. My father bought tickets for the two of us to see Janis Ian at the Main Point, which at the time was the happening folk club in the Philadelphia area. Her song "At Seventeen" was at the top of the charts, and I was in eleventh grade, almost seventeen myself. Going to that concert was one of only a few times I've had my father to myself. When we were kids, our family traveled in a pack. Twosomes were rare and treasured.

What I see when I think about that night is a darkened room with a thick yellow glow around Janis. I liked her show but watching the Beatles and The Jackson Five on a black and white TV had become full color in my mind. Janis's show was the opposite. She was expressing her angst and I could feel her pain. It was the first time I had that experience. I thought songs were something to sing along with or dance to. Listening to Janis changed that.

After college and several more concerts including Billy Joel, Earth, Wind, and Fire, Chicago, and The Pointer Sisters, I had upfront seats for King Crimson at the Mann Music Center in Fairmount

Park. Their album *Discipline* had just come out and I knew all the songs by heart. It was the first time I saw Tony Levin play.

He stood stage right with his Chapman Stick—a 12-string electric instrument with both guitar and bass strings on it. It was strapped to his chest like it was part of him. Six-foot-four, broad and sturdy, he stood with his feet a yard apart like a living compass. His black leather Doc Martin's didn't budge even though his upper body was pulsing. His bass notes were deep and driving. I could feel them in my chest as though they were pounding into me and pulling me out.

My crush on Tony wasn't romantic, though. I didn't want to be a groupie or wait outside the stage door to meet him. I wanted to play music with him. I wanted his brilliance to confirm that the songs I was just beginning to write were brilliant too. He'd played with so many of the musicians I was listening to: Peter Gabriel, Paul Simon, John Lennon. He was everywhere I wanted to be. But I had no idea how to get there.

Ten years later, still dreaming and still unsure, I moved to Woodstock. There were lots of reasons, but in the back of my mind I knew Tony lived there too. Being nearby would increase my odds of getting to play with him.

After my first album came out eighteen months later, I moved to a new place on the other side of town. A few weeks later, UPS left two big packages on my back porch. They were addressed to Tony Levin at the house across the street.

My heart started to pound. I had no idea he lived there.

I couldn't decide what to do.

The thought of knocking on his door terrified me. What would I say? What would I wear?

What I really wanted to do was act like a normal person, but I didn't feel normal at all. I had to get this opportunity right and I didn't have much time to figure how to do that. It was as if my entire career and maybe even my life depended on it. I got his phone number from a friend and called as soon as I could control my breathing. Thankfully he wasn't home. I left a message on his machine. He called back that afternoon and left a message on mine.

"Thanks for calling, Bar."

He said my name like he already knew it!

When I saw his red Jetta pull out an hour later, I left the packages on his porch. He called to thank me but got my machine again. We hadn't met or spoken directly but I was acutely aware of him. I did everything I could to cross his path. I walked around our wooded cul de sac hoping he'd drive by and stop to say hello. When I washed the dishes, I noticed when he went out, curious if there was a pattern that would indicate when I should take my walks.

On the last night of the Second Woodstock concert in 1994, I knew he'd be going out. Peter Gabriel was closing the show and Tony was in the band. I turned my lights out on the second floor so I could look out the window without him seeing me. I pulled up a chair and waited. Finally, at 8:30 as the sun was going down, I heard his motorcycle revving up. Within seconds he was rumbling down the street and gone.

I felt left behind. I wanted to go with him. I wanted to be in the band. I was thirty-five years old and my childhood fantasies were as alive as ever.

I finally met Tony face-to-face at the Woodstock post office. He was walking in as I was walking out.

"Tony!" I said. "It's nice to see you. I'm Bar from

across the street." He seemed to know that already.

"Hey, it's nice to meet you finally."

He was so tall.

"I've been thinking about calling you," I said. That was generally true, but I didn't have a specific reason for calling him. "I keep wondering if you'd be willing to record with me some time?"

"I'd love to," he said.

Holy shit! I thought, trying to keep the grown-up part of me steady.

"That would so great," I said. "I'd love to hear what you'd do with this song of mine." I could hardly believe I was talking to him.

"Just call me when you're ready. You've got my number, I think?"

It was as easy as that! Tony Levin and I were going to record together.

My sundress was soaking when I got to my car.

The song I wanted Tony to play on was "Write Me a Love Letter." It's a quirky song with lots of space and an unusual form, the kind of song he does brilliant things with. So even though I'd already recorded a version of it a year earlier, I wanted to do it again. And because it was a song I could play well,

I figured I wouldn't be immobilized with fear when we got in the studio together.

I called him the next day to figure out how to pull it together.

After a nervous hello on my part and a fully confident one on his, I said, "What's the best way to do this?" I was imagining Bearsville Studio where Dylan recorded, or Dreamland where the B52s and The Band had recorded, both within a few miles of us. Instead, he said, "Just give me the master when you've got your piano part recorded. I'll record my part at home when I have some free time."

He was talking about recording separately. My eyes welled up. There would be no melding of the minds.

"It's the only way I can record tracks for people these days," he said. "I have to do it in between my other work. But don't worry."

Had he heard my heart sink?

"If you don't like what I've played I can always do it again."

Do it again?

Could I ever tell Tony Levin that I didn't like what he played? It was hard enough to tell him there were packages for him on my back porch.

But there was another problem: If I wasn't in the studio with him, he would decide what to play, not me. It was not the way I wanted this to go. I wanted to work with him. I wanted to be in control. I wanted the experience of hearing my song come to life and I wanted to feel what it was like to watch Tony play up close. I wanted everything. But Tony Levin was a god and I was a little girl in awe. I had no choice. If I wanted to hear what he would play, I would have to do it his way.

As soon as I had the piano part recorded—virtually the same part I'd played on the original track—I called Tony again. He suggested I drop the tape at his house to be sure it got to him safely. "I'm home this afternoon if that works for you."

When I got there, I lost my breath again standing alone with him in his living room babbling on about nothing. My tongue was sticky in my mouth and I couldn't make eye contact. He stood in the doorway and listened. When his girlfriend called, I let myself out, relieved that it was over, wishing I was someone else.

Two days later he called and left a message that

he was done, that he'd leave the master tape on his back porch for me to pick up. He also said he loved the song. I could hardly wait to hear it, but I waited to go over until his car was gone.

When I heard what he played I panicked. I didn't like it. I'd gotten so used to the other version that I couldn't adjust to Tony's. Thankfully I didn't call him right away.

I spent the next day listening to his track over and over again trying to figure out how to tell him it wasn't working for me. But by the end of the day my mind had changed. Tony had understood the lyric and had brought my words to life in the same way a soundtrack brings a movie to life. He'd colored the song with the confusion and desperation I'd felt when I wrote it.

I wanted the song to describe the time between relationships, when feelings and questions linger; when it's not love anymore but something else: Desperation. Uncertainty. Confusion. Jealousy. I had been in the midst of those feelings when the song poured out of me. He had captured that.

Tony ended up playing on a lot of my songs in the years that followed, but I still haven't gotten over the thrill of it. And I still can't talk to him without losing my breath.

Write Me A Love Letter

I want to hear your voice and touch your hand
lie down and hear the beating of your heart in my ear
If I could see you I would know where you are
Instead I'm hoping that you'll
write me a love letter, tell me how you feel
write me a love letter, tell me you love me still

So many thoughts are running 'round in my head at night
with him beside me and her face allied with yours
not mine
Every night when the darkness sets in
I lie here wishin' that you'd
write me a love letter, tell me how you feel
write me a love letter, tell me you love me still

Our ending had come in my heart so I turned away
In time I thought you'd change
ease the pain
So won't you write me, tell me how you feel
write me a love letter, tell me you love me

Alone again
I am alone again
Don't turn me away, don't turn me away

Please write me, tell me how you feel
write me a love letter, tell me you love me still

I want to hear your voice and your hand
Lie down and hear the beating of your heart
in my ear

• Mother Love •

The Ways of Water

The bed and breakfast was only partially full. It was the beginning of January and not many people wanted to be at the beach in Ocean Grove, New Jersey at that time of year. I'd been a guest at The Ocean View a couple of times before—once for a month when I wrote the first draft of my memoir, *The Present Giver*, and then again when I was finishing a song called "More." I knew the staff pretty well by then.

At teatime on that Sunday afternoon, one of the other guests introduced himself as Max, a violinist, new to America from Hungary. He'd heard I was singer. He asked me how to get a gig in the U.S. I said, "The only thing I can suggest is to produce your own." I'd just finished a string of house concerts on the east coast and liked them so much I wasn't sure if I'd ever sing in a public venue again. People listened, there was homemade food, a place to stay with a decent bed, and I was paid too. On top of that, I got new fans through old friends and we all had a good time. Max was interested, so I said, "Ya know, we could even do a concert in this hotel." The innkeeper was within earshot and said, "I love that idea! Let's do it." Within the hour, Xeroxed copies of a simple poster were taped to the doors of the hotel buildings. Registered guests and their friends were invited for wine and a concert, and it was free. Everyone was asked to bring a story of their own to share.

The following night, thirteen people assembled around an out-of-tune piano in the main living room. Among them was a round and bubbly woman named Cathy whose father had been offered two camels for her when they were visiting Egypt years before. Max, the violinist, was Cathy's fiancé. They'd met on a cruise ship the previous summer. She was sailing. He was in the orchestra. He played three energetic Gypsy tunes for us, and he spoke a little Hungarian too.

The innkeeper, Angela, told us she was an immigrant from Poland and that her first job in the United States was cleaning offices at night on the upper floors of a skyscraper in New York City. She'd convinced herself that the odd-looking boxes on all the desks were cameras that followed her around to make sure she did her job. She dressed for those cameras hoping one of the security guards who was monitoring her would make a good match. She was horrified when an employee who had stayed late one night jammed a pencil into the center of the camera to sharpen it, dashing all of her dreams.

There was a carpenter, too. He told us he wanted to be a dancer, so he improvised a ballet. He and his boyfriend were celebrating their first night out.

And there was a State Trooper. A man named Roger who told us he was in the doghouse. His wife had given him two months to rearrange his priorities.

All these stories were told one at a time, like campers around a campfire. We didn't know one another when we started, but like people who meet on a plane and tell each other things they haven't told anyone else, we knew each other well by the end of the evening.

My contribution was to sing "More," the song I'd finished at that hotel years before. I wanted to see how people I didn't know would react to it.

"I don't usually write love songs," I told them, "but this is a song about loving someone so much there aren't words to describe it."

The room was dark with just a few leftover holiday candles flickering on the side tables. Christmas lights on the outside of the doors and windows gave the room a gentle glow. It felt like a movie set, like something dramatic and exceptional was happening. There was romance and nostalgia in the air.

"I didn't know how to describe the love I felt so I made a list of things I had loved most in my life. Most were memories, not things at all. I thought if I sang about all them and said I love these things, but I love *you* even more, my point would be made."

The room was quiet as I started to play.

At the end of the night as everyone was getting ready to leave, Roger, the state trooper with an angry spouse, approached me and said, "I wish I could write words like yours. I'd send them to my wife."

His eyes were bright. He smiled as though he knew how corny he sounded.

"You can give her mine if you want. Just tell her you wrote them," I said.

We both laughed knowing that wasn't the answer. When I thought about it later, I wondered if what he really meant to say was that he wished he loved his wife as much as I loved the person I was singing to. I didn't tell him about Forrest.

In the summer our family went to New Hampshire where my grandparents had a house on Lake Winnipesaukee. Every morning, my grandfather would go out to the dock at sunrise and slide into the water for a swim. If I were lucky enough to be up by then, I'd go with him. I loved the quiet, the light browns and yellows of the sun reflecting on the lake. More than anything I loved the feel of the water on my skin—cold, silky, endless.

As I got older, I swam alone at night. I'd sneak out to the dock after everyone had gone to bed, undress, and drop down the ladder to the lake. My eyes, ears, and skin felt every detail on those nights. Coolness. Wetness. The sound of water lapping against the shore. Any splash I made could be heard anywhere around the lake. There were stars or no stars. Clouds or no clouds. And if a full moon was hanging low in the sky, I could swim in the golden light it cast across the water.

This place in New Hampshire that I called Long Lake in my lyric, still appears regularly in my dreams. It's a place of safety, comfort, and contentment.

I love you more than the moonlight on Long Lake
or her water on my skin

When Forrest was born, we read to him at night then I'd nurse him as he fell asleep. I ended every day with, "I love you, Forrest, more than the sky. No matter where you go, no matter what you do, I will always love you." Before he got sick, my words were a reminder to him, permission for him to go out and explore his life with my unconditional support. After cancer took hold, the words had new meaning.

Saying, "no matter where you go" no longer meant a place on Earth like Manhattan or Boise. It meant somewhere unknown. It meant the hereafter, wherever that was. They were hard words to say every night, but I needed to say them. I needed the hope that they could still mean Boise, while accepting the fact that they probably meant the hereafter. It was a nightly reminder of the beauty and mystery of life and death, which at the time I was obsessed with. I still say these words every now and then hoping Forrest can hear me.

For years afterwards I could see the Hudson Valley as the sun rose in the east every morning through the windows at the foot of our bed: pinks, blues, oranges, gold, and purple or gray. The colors and the sureness of the sun's ascent were a daily comfort in Forrest's absence.

As was sleep.

Sleep was a time when I might see Forrest again. His visits in my dreams were rare, and often stressful. He might be dying again, he might be lost where I couldn't find him or in a place I couldn't reach, but at least I could see him. I could feel him. I couldn't wait for sleep. And I was so glad that the terror of waiting for his death was over.

I love you more than the sky as daylight breaks
from the darkness that was night
Glorious night!

Growing up, my parents' room was on the third floor under the eaves. My four older sisters, younger brother and I slept on the second floor in groups of two until Billy got his own room. On Christmas mornings, we were up at first light, anxious to see what Santa had delivered. But there were rules: no going downstairs until everyone was up, and no peeking. My parents, having been up late, were slow to get moving, so when the tension got too great, we'd scurry up the stairs and pile up on top of them until they'd give in. When they finally got moving, we'd all go back down to the very last stair we were allowed to sit on, the one just before the turn in the stair that led to the living room where all the presents were. My father would always have to brush his teeth first making the wait unbearable, until finally, all the world was magic and wrapping paper.

I love you more than the joy of Christmas morning and the lights up on the tree

One of those Christmases I got my first "big" present. These were presents that were special—maybe a bike or a bookcase. In my case, it was a Zenith compact stereo with a turntable that held five LPs on a spindle, and speakers that folded into the middle like the Barbie dollhouse I got at the church fair. Having my own stereo was huge. Crosby, Stills, Nash and Young had come out with *Deja Vu*, James Taylor with *Sweet Baby James*, and McCartney with *Ram*—all albums I still have.

Two of my older sisters had gone to college by then so I had my own room and could listen to whatever I wanted for as long as I wanted. Three Dog Night's "Joy to the World" and Blood, Sweat, and Tears' "Spinning Wheel" were the first two songs I learned by heart in that room. On the rare occasion when I was the only one home, I'd pack up the stereo and take it down to the living room where we had a small grand piano. I'd try to play along with "Let it Be." It's still one of my favorite songs ever.

I never told anyone about any of that. I'm not

sure why. If I had, my mother would have suggested lessons. It's as if I liked the thrill of my secret more than the playing. It was mine. No one could tamper with it or trespass on it if they didn't know how much I loved it. It took ten years for those longings to express themselves; ten more until I was making my own albums and coloring in the details of my dreams.

I love you more than the colors of the night.
when I close my eyes and my dreams come to life

One of my favorite memories is of Forrest standing at the window in our bedroom looking out at the falling snow. He was bouncing on his toes, smiling, "Look, Mommy, it's snowing!" It had been falling all night and everything was white. His tiny fingers were on the windowsill. He could hardly wait to get outside. Remembering it filled me with the same kind of joy. I wanted the bridge of my song to capture that memory, and the miracle that Forrest had been here at all.

When winter comes
and water forms in sheets and icicles
one snowflake falling a miracle in flight
and when the morning comes and all is white
I love you more

There was water everywhere in the song I was writing—tears, rain, icicles, snow, water from the lake on my skin—but I hadn't seen any of it until my second trip to Ocean Grove, five years before we did our living room concert at The Ocean View.

I'd gone to the beach to find the words to the chorus of my new song. A lyric, I hoped, would pull the song together. The sun was out. The beach was empty. It was October, the month I like best by the ocean. It was warm enough to go barefoot with my pants rolled up. I walked where the sand was hard, at the place where the waves turn around and go back to the ocean. This was a place where I always felt whole and good, where any sadness or worries I had fell away. I felt sure that while I was there the words would come, and they did.

More

*More than the moonlight on Long Lake
or her water on my skin
I love you more than the sky as daylight breaks
from the darkness that was night, glorious night!
The sound of waves and sand beneath my feet
        As far as my eyes will ever see*

*I love you more than the joy of Christmas morning
and the lights up on the tree.
I love you more than the colors of the night
when I close my eyes and my dreams come to life*

        *In pouring rain with pools around my feet
        and soft summer rain that cools the heat
        I love you more*

*When winter comes
and water forms in sheets and icicle
one snowflake falling a miracle in flight.
and when the morning comes and all is white
I love you more*

        *The sound of waves and sand beneath my feet
        In all that I see*

FINDING A WAY

You are to me
I love you more

• Education •

Singing With Others

Rhinebeck's Center for Performing Arts in upstate, New York is a modern, cavernous place. There's no raised stage, no proscenium arch, no curtains or orchestra pit. The movie-theater-style seats rise steeply in rows from the floor to the rafters. Catwalks, lighting trusses, and air conditioning vents are visible from below.

The night I played there two other performers were playing too. We were the first in an on-going series featuring up-and-coming singer-songwriters. An hour before the show, the stage manager told us they'd only sold twenty tickets. The theater held 300.

No one was surprised. People don't like to go out to hear someone they've never heard of before.

"On nights like this," the manager said, "we give kids from the local halfway house tickets to see the show. It's good for them, and it fills seats." All I could think was, *these kids are gonna hate my music.* They'd be bored, too, which was even worse.

After the stage manager left, I told Jen and Erica who were singing with me that night that we'd need to re-think our set. The halfway kids were teenagers. I was convinced they'd want to hear music that was as far from what I was offering as possible. We had to come up with songs they'd like. I picked the few up-tempo songs I'd written thinking they'd have the best shot of winning the kids over.

My friend John Erickson started the show. I felt sorry for him. He was alone with his acoustic guitar singing songs inspired by Dan Fogelberg. In my mind, his songs were as lightweight as mine. Not the kind of music tough teenagers would want to listen to. From where I was sitting off stage, I could see the mostly empty seats. In the farthest back corner to my left the halfway kids sat together in a thick pile. Legs were hung over seats, heads were down, hands were covering eyes like this was the worst night of their lives. They slapped each other on the arm and giggled amongst themselves when something they heard was annoying or funny. I imagined them rolling their eyes each time John started a new song. I was scared to do my show, but I had to.

Just before we went on stage, though, I had a change of heart. I turned to Jen and Erica and said, "Forget it. We're playing what we came to play." I had a hunch no matter what we did the kids were going to ignore us.

The people with tickets sat front and center. They were within a few feet of me when I got to the piano. I was glad they were there. When I sat down, I felt like the piano protected me from the hostile eyes I imagined to be peering down at me from the last rows. I was safe there. We played a few songs and got the same response John had gotten from the kids. After a couple more, I got up from the piano to sing acapella with Jen and Erica. I was vulnerable now, standing by myself without a piano to hide behind.

"This is one of the first songs I ever wrote," I told

the audience. "It's called 'His Mother's Legacy.' It grew out of a mistake I made."

In the early '80s, the release of digital synthesizers made it possible for musicians to record a part with a piano, for instance, and then experiment with what it would sound like if the part were played by an organ or a trumpet. I had recorded a piano part but then I'd inadvertently caused the keyboard to play the same part as a conga. As soon as I heard drums, I started to sing. It was a whole new piece and I loved it.

"That mistake," I told the audience, "has always reminded me of Mr. Donald. He was the principle at my junior high. When I was getting a D in Biology, he told my mom not to worry because I didn't *need* biology. I loved him for that. Another time he called the whole school in for an assembly. Somebody had gotten in trouble for something I can't remember. He wanted the rest of us to understand that everyone makes mistakes, that we should learn from them and not make the same one twice."

While I was telling the audience about my D in biology and Mr. Donald's assembly, the kids got quieter. They weren't hiding under their hoodies anymore. They were listening. "I'm not a parent yet," I said, "but this song is about the one thing I would teach my son if I thought I could teach him anything. Someday I want my kids to know I'll love them regardless of what they do or the mistakes they make." It was the kind of parent I wanted to be.

I sang the first verse by myself: *listen, my son/your life is all that I can give/If I could I'd teach you all that I have learned/Go and err, and know my love.* The second time through, Jen joined me on djembe and a harmony vocal, then Erica came in a few lines later. Our lyrics repeated over and over again in a round.

Midway through I heard commotion in the back of the theater. The kids were moving around. I could hear their voices. They were leaning into one another, making percussion sounds with their mouths. They got louder and louder, more courageous. Their energy caused ours to intensify. We were in conversation with them and it was electric. The people in the front rows didn't know where to look. Some of them closed their eyes and smiled, some of them twisted around to watch. It went on like that for several minutes before Jen and Erica's voices dropped out one after the other. Then the kids' voices and mine got quieter until the djembe and their voices were all that was left.

His Mother's Legacy

Listen my son
Your life is all that I can give

If I could I'd teach you all that I have learned

Go and err
And know my love
And know my love is in your heart

• Innocence •

Before and After

I was sitting at my piano in Woodstock when I played a phrase that held my attention for the next several hours. This is how songs get started for me. I played my new melody over and over again. It was different from anything I'd played before. The opening chords clashed and resolved, then clashed and resolved again. My earlier piano melodies had almost always sounded simple. Pretty. This one was nuanced, a little dissonant. I felt like a pianist for the first time. I didn't know I could play so well. This was a real piece of music. Not just something to sing along with. I was mesmerized and couldn't stop. If I did the magic would end and I'd lose my chance. I stuck with it for the rest of the day, tape recorder nearby to catch my work as it progressed.

I called the song "Heaven" from the start. I don't know why. I played it for weeks until I was sure I wouldn't forget the form. I didn't have lyrics, but I had a melody, so I hummed along, singing random words here and there. Singers call this vocalizing. We do it when we warm up, but we also do it if we're songwriters and we're searching for words to a new song. I've learned to trust the sounds I make unconsciously. They often suggest lyrics that teach me something about myself.

It happened when I wrote "I'm Here" for my soon-to-be husband Peter a couple of years earlier. I had vocalized a line that sounded something like "my heart cried out." So I asked myself what's your heart crying out for? And before I had time to think about it, the word me came to mind. My heart was crying out for me. I was thirty-six years old. I'd always adjusted too much: said yes when I was too insecure to say no; opened my heart too wide when others didn't want my heart to be so open, or they weren't willing to open their own. The final lyric was my heart cried out for loving that only I could give. Until I wrote that, I didn't know I was having trouble loving myself; that not loving myself had a lot to do with why earlier relationships hadn't worked.

The piano part for "Heaven" came easily, but the lyrics took work and an almost complete preoccupation with the song for months. Even then, I had no clear sense of what I wanted to say. Finally, I decided to play the piano part at a concert in Peter's hometown. I was comfortable there. The audience was full of familiar faces: Peter's family, friends, and people who had heard me sing before.
Late in the show when it came time to introduce "Heaven," I said, "I want to play a new song for you, but I don't have lyrics yet." Everyone laughed as if this were normal.

"If anything comes to mind while you're listening, let me know. Maybe it'll help me get the lyrics." They laughed again until the room was quiet.

When I played the last chord nearly five minutes later, I held the keys down until the sound of the piano disappeared into silence. Sometimes music feels like a place. A location I can go to. That's how

"Heaven" felt that night.

After the show Peter's cousin Mary told me she'd imagined children playing when she heard the music. "They were running around, falling down and enjoying themselves," she said, "but I had the feeling that something bad was going to happen."

I'd imagined children playing too, but when Mary described foreboding, I thought of my childhood friend Donna. Her older sister Susan had been killed instantly when a metal bar on a May Pole struck her in the head. Donna was an infant at the time. Her mother watched as it happened. When Donna told me about Susan years later, we were ten or eleven. It made a big impression on me. I hadn't experienced death yet.

As I worked on my lyrics, I realized Donna's mother had become a whole new person when Susan fell. From that moment on there was a before and an after.

People often ask if I write the music or lyrics first. For me, lyrics always come last and I usually need a deadline to get them finished. The music starts with a phrase or a couple of chords that sound good together. I record any short snippet of music I play that holds my attention for more than a few minutes. These aren't recordings that anyone else would want to hear. They're like the doodles or sketches you might draw while you're on the phone. Over time, though, an initial sketch may develop into ten or twenty versions of the same melody. When it's time to make a new album, I'll listen to my audio doodles everywhere I go until the ones I'm most drawn to come into focus. Eventually I sit at the piano or pick up my guitar to figure out what I'd originally played. Often the initial sketch, no matter how crooked, has a quality to it that I want to re-create. I don't read or notate music well, so looking at my scribbled notes is a waste of time. I use my ears to find the melodies and feelings again. Usually my fingers remember. I'm not sure that's a good thing. I wonder if it's because I do the same things over and over again. But then I think of Edgar Degas and all those ballerinas, and I say to myself, it's ok. It's all right if you repeat yourself. Some might even call it style. Telling myself this keeps me from giving up on songs that sound like something I've written before.

When the music is finished, my need to write the

lyrics consumes me. Before then I may have a word or two, maybe a sense of what the song will be about, but not a lot more. The music gives me an environment to sing in. It's an emotional and physical place. I go there and I need to describe it in words. When I have that musical space to sing in, I don't think about much else. I carry paper and pen everywhere I go in case a line or a word comes to mind. This is by far my favorite time of songwriting. It's when I know the song will be finished but I have no idea how. The music becomes a soundtrack to the movie that started in my head the first time I played the melody. Images start to form, action takes place, and characters come to life. In the case of "Heaven" I saw children playing in my head just like Peter's cousin Mary did. I didn't know why yet, but I wanted to follow them. I saw little girls in patent leather Mary Janes wearing cotton dresses with smocking across the chest. They wore little white socks like the ones I used to wear. The boys wore brown suede shoes, plaid cotton shirts, and suspenders on their jeans. They ran in circles singing "Ring Around the Rosie." They laughed, fell down, and got up again.

Later in my internal movie, one of the girls is

older. She's lying on her back in tall grass. One of the boys is with her but I don't see him. She's wearing a denim skirt and a loose cotton blouse. She's preoccupied with the movement of the clouds above her. She seems distracted as though she's not sure she wants to be there. Something has happened that she doesn't understand, but I don't know what that is. Then I see her on her knees. Is she praying? Why is she on her knees? The boy is standing nearby. He's smiling as though he's won something. What is it? And then it hits me: I know why she's on her knees, and I know why she feels lost.

This movie I've created in my head is not a memory. This is not something that happened to me that I want to write a song about. The characters have a life of their own, but I'm creating them, which makes me wonder why. They're like dreams that way. I look for lyrics that describe what's happening in my film. I know I've got the right ones when I sing the words and my film runs with no interruptions. That's when I know I've gotten to the essence of the song. It may take a long time, though, before I understand it. In the case of "Heaven" that was years.

I finished writing "Heaven" in 1997 before Forrest was conceived. I recorded it in 2000. Three weeks later, Forrest was diagnosed.

I was asked to sing "Heaven" at the memorial for the first-year anniversary of 9-11 at The Woodstock Playhouse in 2002. The theater was full. Musicians and clergy sat in a single line across the stage, waiting their turn to speak or sing. The night air in the open amphitheater was clear and cool. Because Forrest had died six months earlier, and because the song was fairly new, people thought I was singing about him. To this day they think so, and in many ways I am.

Heaven

*Years ago I remember holding hands
running around and falling down
In circles then, the sun was shining everywhere
I remember my hand in your hand
and then I find that I remember holding you
in the grass in the meadow
and here I am, I'm on my knees*

*Looking to heaven so far away
searching for my way*

*In love with you
the sun was shining down on my
I remember just lying there
the sky was turning like a movie screen
where the clouds roll in fast
and here I am, I'm on my knees again*

*Looking for heaven, far, far away
so far that I can't find my way*

*When I am here
roses are red, a violet's blue
when I'm in love with you*

When I am here
ashes to ashes
we all fall down
and we get up again
We all get up

    I'm walking all the way to heaven
Heaven here I come
I'm almost all the way to heaven
Heaven turned away

Why am I here?
where roses are red and black
and no violet's blue when I'm in love with you
Why am I here?
ashes to ashes
we all fall down
and we get up again
We all get up

• Relationships •

Grapes and Seeds

I started writing "Love is the Reason" on a friend's out-of-tune spinet. I was visiting. She had gone to work so I had the whole day to myself. Something about being in and unfamiliar place with a different piano inspires me. The change in setting releases new juice in my heart.

 Peter and I had been together for several months by then. We'd been hesitant about one another from the start. Some of that hesitation had stuck. He was still emotionally attached to an old girlfriend, and my old boyfriends were making me question my ability to choose a good partner. I wanted all of them to go away. I wanted to open myself up to Peter, take the risk that he could love all of me, not just the pretty parts he knew about.

While I was writing the lyrics, I realized my fear of sharing myself with Peter was because if I did, I might overwhelm him with my intensity and my seriousness. But I also worried that if I opened myself up too far, I wouldn't be able to stop from sharing every sadness I'd ever felt. That idea scared me even more.

During the ten months we dated we broke up and got back together every month or so. He was so dizzy by the end of that summer that he said, "You're like a squirrel crossing the road. You run out, stop, think, run away, then run back again." It was a good analogy. When the song was done, Peter called the last few lines the squirrel section, so I did too. I was afraid to commit because I was afraid of getting hurt. The song was a prayer for intimacy.

Whenever I sing it, I think of Peter, of course, but I also think of the kitchen on the pediatric floor at Albany Medical. I met my friend Marcy there in the early days of cancer.

It was the go-to place when I needed to hide for a

few minutes. Forrest had been diagnosed six weeks earlier. His odds for survival were tiny. By then he was doing his second round of chemo. I had to find moments alone to pull myself together. I was worried that any weakness I showed would worry Forrest even more. He had already shut down. He wouldn't talk. He lay in a full-sized bed, guarded by metal rails, propped up on pillows, wide-eyed, and watching everything that was going on—nurses checking his pumps, taking his vitals every hour, doctors probing his belly, then more doctors probing his belly. There was no way to explain what was happening to him.

Marcy was hiding in the kitchen too. One of her students was doing chemo. Cheyenne was thirteen. She had cancer in her sinuses. Marcy taught music in the rural Adirondack school where Cheyenne lived. Class sizes ranged from seven to ten students and she'd been Cheyenne's teacher since kindergarten. She was like a grandmother. She came to the hospital to give Cheyenne's mother Doreen a break.

Cheyenne was Cherokee—dark and beautiful with deep brown eyes that looked straight at your heart. She wanted to be a singer when she grew up. To give her a chance at that dream, Marcy set up a karaoke machine in the pediatric floor's playroom one night so Cheyenne could do a concert. Forrest, Doreen, Marcy, Peter, me, and a little boy named Mikey who lived at the hospital, were the audience. Mikey was severely disabled, but joyful despite being abandoned by his parents. His round puffy face had a perpetual smile and his big watery eyes comprehended who knows what.

As Cheyenne sang, Forrest bounced up and down, knees bending more or less to the groove from the karaoke box. He tapped his index fingers on a wooden table as he smiled and stared up at Cheyenne, both of them tethered to IV poles.

A year later I met Marcy again at a memorial weekend held at Paul Newman's Hole in the Wall camp in the Adirondacks. Cheyenne and Forrest had died within a few weeks of one another earlier that year. I'd been asked to sing "Love is the Reason" at a gathering for parents who had lost a child, and then later in the service, "Amazing Grace," which I sang acapella from the center of the room while I held Doreen's hand. Afterwards we all met down by the lake below the mess hall and I sang "Grace" as parents launched tiny sailboats with their child's name crayoned on the sail.

The night I met Marcy in the hospital kitchen sixteen months earlier, she asked for a copy of *Grapes and Seeds*, the album "Love is the Reason" is on, an album I had finished recording just before Forrest got sick. After she heard it, she asked if she could get copies of my other albums. What I didn't know until that day at Paul Newman's camp was that she'd wanted to hear more because she was hoping to find something about my music she would like.

This makes me smile now. She became my most devoted fan in the years that followed. When she died in 2014, I realized how much I'd relied on her faith in my music. I still miss her.

When I saw her sitting alone on the mess hall porch after the memorial service, I went over to sit with her. She was crying. Most of us were, on and off.

"Are you okay?" I asked knowing she wasn't but aware that on that day the question meant something. She couldn't look at me. It was all too much.

Finally, she said, "I just have to thank you." That wasn't what I expected to hear. Tears were streaming down her face. Mine too. "I didn't get it before," she said. "I didn't understand your music or what you were trying to do. But when you sang today, I finally got it. I haven't been able to cry since Cheyenne left and I'm just so thankful."

Of all the things people have said about my music over the years, Marcy's is the dearest. You just never know when something you do will help someone else.

Love is the Reason

I have caught my emotions right down under my skin
Come, my love, lie out in the open and I'll let you in
I'll try

I'll find all the bruises. I'll touch every scar
I will make no excuses
I'll feed you grapes and seeds and love
Love is the reason I love this life

If I started to show you, I may never stop
When I try to free my emotions
I feed you grapes and seeds and love

You and I believe in the other side of love
All we really need for the other side is love
If I turn to you, I might run away
turn around, then run back again
Oh, Love

· Judgment ·

Willy and Me

I met Willy in 1988 at a friend's party in downtown Philadelphia. He looked like Clint Eastwood without the height or the cowboy boots. I fell for him immediately. Problem was, I was moving to New York City two weeks later.

We commuted—or rather *I* commuted—back and forth to see each other every other weekend. He played tennis on Saturdays and was reluctant to miss a match. This went on for a long time without a lightbulb going on in my head.

At dinner six months into the relationship, I learned that Willy and his roommate were headed to

Australia the following week.

Australia? Willy hadn't mentioned a trip to Australia. When his roommate brought it up, Willy acted like he'd been caught in a trap. He'd been hiding something, and it wasn't a girlfriend. Willy had a guru. He told me later that night that he hadn't told me because he didn't think I'd understand. He had been following the guru around the world for over twenty years. He had lived on an ashram in India for thirteen until a few months before we met. It was a pretty big detail to withhold. I should have gotten back on a train to New York that very night, and not because of the guru. Instead, I told myself I was being judgmental. I spent another year trying to understand.

I went to meetings in Manhattan where the guru arrived by video, piloting the private jet his followers provided. All around me, acolytes swooned in their seats, imagining the guru sitting in a well-lit but empty chair on center stage. From the screen on the left he talked about love and finding inner peace through meditation. I couldn't sit still. I was angry. I wanted Willy to come over to my side. See what I saw. Understand that he wasn't getting the guru's message. He hadn't learned how to love at all. He certainly wasn't loving me the way I wanted to be loved. The guru was in his way. I didn't think there was room for me in his heart. The guru was taking up too much space.

It wasn't until I heard an interview with Paul McCartney almost thirty years later that I understood what I was really writing about when I wrote my song about Willy.

Stephen Colbert asked McCartney if he thought his mother's death when he was fourteen had affected the musician he'd become. *Of course it did*, I thought to myself. But McCartney said he didn't think it had affected him musically until years later. People kept telling him that "Yesterday" was a song about his mom. He choked up as he talked about it. Then he broke a line of the lyrics into three separate lines with a question mark at the end of each:

"Why she had to go"?

"I don't know"?

"She wouldn't say"?

Then he talked about how he didn't mean for the song to be about his mom.

In the same way, my lyrics about Willy describe

everything *I* was going through at the time—moving to New York City, searching for something I wasn't sure of, questioning myself at every turn, looking for answers, wanting what I had with Willy to be love. I may have been describing my frustration with him and his guru, but I was talking about myself.

Oh Willy, Love is All

You run away from everything, you run too far
Wonder if you know what you're missin'
wonder if you see

I don't know how the world is turnin'
I don't know why
Turn the outside into the middle
Turn the inside out
Oh Willy, there's nothin' like time to remind you
Oh Willy, love is all

Don't run away from everything, don't run so far
If nothing' seems to fit when you're tryin'
nothin' seems to fit
Oh Willy, nothin' like time to remind you
Oh Willy, love is all

Don't know where to find it,
don't know where to look
I just can't find it

• Comparisons •

My Old Man

When I moved to Woodstock from New York City in 1992, I felt sure the mountain air, the quiet nights, and the musicians and artists nearby would fill me with inspiration. I'd recorded my first album by then and looked forward to writing new songs with more depth and maturity.

Instead, I couldn't write a thing.

I'd sit at the piano or pick up my guitar, but nothing happened. I had everything I needed but nothing to say.

Around that time, I began to imagine an old man every time I sat down to play. He wore white robes with a rope around his waist. His hair and beard were white, long, and flowing. He looked like a shepherd out of a pastoral elegy. He was everything I wanted to be—wise, creative, original, but more than anything, content. He wasn't worried about a new album or meeting the right people.

At first my old man inspired me, but with time I began to compare myself to him. Nothing I did was good enough or worthy of his attention. I had to get rid of him if I wanted to get anything done. To do that, I wrote a song about him.

At a writing workshop a few years later, I read the lyrics of the song to a group of writers who had come to learn something about songwriting. Their response was tepid. What I wanted them to understand is that with songwriting, the music does a lot of the work. When I put the words and music together their response was entirely different. They were quiet, attentive, emotional by the time I finished. We all knew about having someone in our head reminding us that our writing isn't good enough. Writing a song about my old man showed me how many obstacles I'd put in my own way.

Comparing myself to an idealized man was a big one; so was forgetting the beauty of imperfection.

Up on the Hill

Nothing seems to bother him
Nothing is so real
as the leaves on the tree up on the hill
By night he sleeps so easily
then by day, he roams the hill
On his way past the tree
He hears birds while they sing

And the leaves that form slowly after winter
will later fall silent to the ground

Nothing seems so far away
Nothing is so dear
as the leaves on the tree up on the hill
I've put gates, forks and barriers
all along the wooded lane
that leads through the trees
past the birds while they sing

And the leaves that form slowly after winter
will later fall silent to the ground
Nothing seems to bother him
Nothing is so real
as the leaves on the tree up on the hill

FINDING A WAY

He sees every leaf so clearly
He sees the forest from the trees

Why can't it be me that I see
when I sit up on the hill?

'cause the leaves that form slowly after winter
will later fall silent to the ground
The leaves that form so slowly after winter
will later fall silent to the ground

· Hope ·

Here and There

I saw Peter for the first time on Halloween in 1993. It was early afternoon. He was shopping in the produce aisle at Sunflower Natural Foods in Woodstock. I noticed his red hair, his beard, and his well-worn, knee-length brown leather coat. He looked good. He smiled when he caught me looking at him. That's when I noticed his light blue eyes.

When I was done shopping, I walked to my car, hoping he'd come out behind me, but he didn't. From my car, I watched for him in my rearview mirror. A few minutes later he walked out and got into a white van with Shokan Electric written in big black letters on the side. As he did, I said out loud to myself, "There's no way I'm marrying an electrician." I was tired of boyfriends who didn't have enough money to take me to dinner every so often. I figured a guy who worked for an electrical contractor probably didn't have much either.

The following week I got a call from someone who hung up on me as soon as I said hello. Ten minutes later the phone rang again. When I picked it up the voice said, "Is this Bar Scott?"

"It is," I said as though I was my own receptionist, "but could you call back in a few minutes? I'm on another call." I didn't realize I was torturing my future husband. I figured whoever was calling was looking for money and wouldn't try again.

But half-an-hour later the phone rang again. "Hello. Is this Bar Scott the singer?"

This time, the question made me curious and a little nervous too. It might be a work call, but it might also be an over-enthusiastic fan. My "yes" had an edge to it.

"My name is Peter. We saw each other in town last week and I needed to call you. We made pretty strong eye contact."

I was inclined to hang up, but I didn't. "That couldn't have been me," I said, "I have a boyfriend." I'd been dating someone but mostly I was looking for a way to get off the phone.

Peter was not giving up. "It was Halloween, right before the parade. We were at Sunflower. That wasn't you?"

And with that, he had me. I started to laugh because what else could I do? By the end of our conversation forty-five minutes later I learned that he was from Philadelphia too, that he was the youngest of six children, that he loved music, owned Shokan Electric, and lived five miles away from me on the other side of town. Before we hung up, he said, "Well, that was fun. When we see each other on the street now we can laugh about how we met."

"No," I said, ignoring the other boyfriend. "Let's get together anyway."

The following Saturday morning we talked for two more hours at Maria's Bazaar, a coffee shop in the center of town. A year later, we were married.

I'm Here

I thought that love was hiding in the stars above
My heart was ice from trying to find it in the dark

Now I'm here to take a load off your feet
I'm here to make your kisses complete
I'm here to learn a lesson in how to love

My heart cried out for loving that only I could give
I heard her cry and listened as I turned within

Now I'm here when the crossroads meet
I'm here when the river runs deep
I'm here to learn a lesson in how to love

And as the stars set in your eyes
I see the love I'd tried to find
Sometimes we look so far

but loving starts if I am here
to take a load off your feet
I'm here to make your kisses complete
I'm here to learn a lesson in how to love

And as the stars set in your eyes

FINDING A WAY

I see the love I'd tried to find
Sometimes we look so far
but loving starts if I am here
to take a load off your feet
I'm here to make your kisses complete
I'm here to learn a lesson in how to love you

I love you, Love
I'm glad I'm here

After

• Preparation •

Birthday

When I told Peter I was pregnant, his eyes filled with tears and his mouth twisted up like it always does when he gets emotional. Then he panicked. He'd wanted to have a child, but once it was real, he wondered if he would be a good enough dad. I knew he would be. I was 39. He was 36. We'd been married for three years. The reality was more emotional than either of us had expected. We held each other for a long time and cried.

Forrest was born at 6:38 on August 23rd, 1998. I spent the day before pacing, panting, and selling my hardly-used Taylor cutaway guitar. I'd been advertising it for eight months. No one had called until that morning. When a young man asked if I was the person selling the Taylor, I said yes as another contraction took over my body.

"Could I come see it later today?"

"Umm. It's not a great day for me to show it to you. I'm in labor."

"That's ok," he said, as if I were busy making sandwiches for a picnic that afternoon. "That doesn't bother me." The more insistent he was, the more I realized I might as well sell the guitar. Forrest wasn't coming for at least another ten hours.

"I'm in Troy," he said. "I could be there in two hours."

And he was. He sat on our couch and played for another two as I continued to pace around the house in a nearly see-through cotton dress my sister Mary got in Mexico. He was a really good picker. He bought the guitar. I knew he would. It sounded too good for him to walk away. He didn't ask for a lower price either, just handed me cash, and never said a word about the baby I was about to deliver.

At 10:00 that night, Peter called Mary, our doula. When she got to our house, the lights were turned down and I was playing the piano, crying quietly between contractions. I wasn't in pain, but I was overcome with what was happening. Forrest was part of me already. The rest of my life was unknown, and I was scared, but I couldn't wait to see him. It's hard to write this now. I'd written a lullaby for him and I'd been singing it to him every night for months. I was singing it when Mary got there:

Go to sleep now
it's time to dream
and go to where the angels meet
They'll shower you with kisses
and shelter you from harm
and bring you safely back into my arms

Mary told me I was drifting too far away. She wanted me to snap out of it. My eyes had glazed over and the idea of my body being the vehicle by which Forrest entered the world overwhelmed me with a sense of holiness—his and mine. That's the only way I can describe it. Everything was out of my hands. While I was disappearing into the vastness of what was happening, Mary was coaching me to get back into my body and focus on delivering this baby.

When I wouldn't come back, she worried I would check-out completely. Maybe she thought I was delirious. Maybe I was. At 1:00 we called Jenna, the midwife, and arranged to meet her at the birthing center in Rhinebeck forty-five minutes away.

Jenna met us but went home again feeling sure Forrest wouldn't come until much later in the day. For the rest of the night until Jenna came back at 5:00 in the morning, Mary looked me in the eyes and repeated, "Come back, Bar, come back. Get into your body and push this baby out." I had opted not to have pain medication and was struggling with the intensity of it all.

But when Forrest was on my chest at 6:40 that morning, I'd forgotten the pain. I didn't know until Forrest showed up how much I loved being his mom.

Where the Angels Meet

*Go to sleep now
It's time to dream
and go to where the angels meet
They'll shower you with kisses
and shelter you from harm
and bring you safely back in to my arms*

*They will feed you milk and honey
from streams that flow with love
All around you stars will shine
where the angels meet*

*Go to sleep now
I'll be here when you stir
to start another day with you
Each day I'll wonder!
Each day I'll long to see
the places where your dreams will lead*

*And I will feed you milk and honey
from streams that flow with love
All around you stars will shine
where the angels meet*

So fly away, little one, you're my angel

Go to sleep now
Find your dreams
where the angels meet
Go to where the angels meet
Go to sleep

• Salvation •

Out of the Blue

After Forrest was diagnosed, he got so many presents that the space under my piano became a storage area for blocks, stuffed animal overflow, and yards of plastic train tracks. I kept it clear enough so I could play whenever there was a quiet moment—welcomed respite from motherhood and cancer.

Forrest was playing in the bedroom one day when I thought I could steal a few moments for myself at the piano. Within seconds I was far away, listening to my hands and losing track of time and place. The music was quiet and rolling like a harp. A few minutes later, Forrest came out of the bedroom with a couple of stuffed animals clutched to his chest. He was looking right at me when he said, "Maaah-mee, where arrr you?" I had gotten in the habit of turning my cassette recorder on as soon as I sat down to play, so I caught his sing-songy question on tape. I don't know how I responded, though, because I had turned the recorder off before I answered. Every so often I find that tape and hear Forrest's voice again. "Maaah-mee, where arrr you?" It used to make me cry. But when I hear it now it's as if he's reminding me to pay attention, to not disappear.

On a perfect summer day three years later, the sky was a welcoming blue. You could see for miles. No clouds. No wind. Just openness and a feeling that all was well.

Late in the morning, I felt something I'd never felt before. Lyrics for a song were heading towards me. It was if they'd come together to form a boat that was sailing my way, slow and determined, ready to dock, one word at a time. All I had to do was open the slip and let them in. I sat on the couch in my studio and waited, confident they were on their way. As they arrived, I scribbled them down on lines I'd drawn like parking spots for them to land on. An hour later, there was only one space left.

I waited, but it just didn't come.

Finally, I got up and played the piano part I'd written for the song months earlier, hoping the final word would slip out when I wasn't trying so hard. When that didn't work, I lay on the floor to stretch. I'd painted a mural of the sky on the ceiling—billowing teal clouds around the perimeter and soft white in the center. I often lay there pretending my painted sky was a portal to wherever Forrest was. I imagined him looking down at me lying on the floor, wondering what I was doing, wishing he could lie there with me.

I sang as I searched my painted sky. Then out of the blue a parachute came into view.

A parachute.

It was all Forrest needed to get home, and all I needed to land safely in my new life.

Parachute

Here's where I'm gonna be
There's where you're gonna be
Parachute

If you were here with me
I wouldn't need to go home

Up above the air is filled with perfect sky
clouds of pink and blue
and some as pure as white

There's where I'm gonna be
Will you be there for me?
Parachute

Here, in the center of the great unknown
Here where the seeds of life have always grown
It's hard to be alone

Here's where I'm gonna be
Here's where I'd rather be
Here, with you

If it could only be I'd like for you to come home

FINDING A WAY

Up above the air is filled with perfect sky
clouds of pink and blue
and some as pure as white
Here, in the center of the great unknown
Here where the seed of life in me has grown
I like to be alone

Come on now Parachute hold on tight and pull the
shoot come on now just parachute hold on tight and
pull the shoot come on now don't be afraid to parachute
back to me

Here, in the center of the great unknown
Here I am
I am

• Harmony •

Anatomy of a Song

Set the World on Fire

Introduction

Once I start playing "Set the World on Fire," I can't wait to sing the first verse, especially if my friend Kirsti is singing with me. It's as if a bunch of little kids I used to know are coming back to life.

Verse 1

When Hurricane Harvey moved through Woodstock in 1999, Peter, Forrest, and I went out on the front deck to watch. Forrest had always loved the wind, especially coming up our driveway—me holding him tight, his body halfway out the window. As Harvey moved towards us, I held Forrest by the waist. He leaned into the wind with his little-boy feet steady on the railing. He was like Kate Winslett and Leonardo DiCaprio on the bow of the Titanic. Intoxicated. Content. Ready for whatever might come next.

Chorus

It was Christmastime 2001 when we discovered the video adaptation of Raymond Briggs' picturebook, *The Snowman.* There's no dialogue, just Briggs' pastel drawings of a snowman coming to life, and the orchestral soundtrack by Howard Blake. The single voice we hear in the film is Peter Auty's, who at the time was a soprano in the boys' choir at Saint Paul's Cathedral in London. The snowman has taken the hand of the little boy who is dreaming him. Auty's voice soars as the two of them fly over continents, oceans, and snow-topped mountains, until finally, they arrive at Santa's workshop at the North Pole.

Every time Forrest heard Auty's voice, he'd stop what he was doing, focus on the TV, then start to hum. It always made me stop too. I watched Forrest knowing he still had mountains to climb.

Whenever I pushed Forrest on the swings, he would say, "To the clouds, mommy!" then squeal with delight as his body swung down to the earth, then back up to the sky.

Verse 2

Every February at Supertots, Forrest's teacher Cheryl transformed her classroom into a beach. She'd cover the purple rug with a big plastic tarp, spread out a little sand, put a ten-foot pool on top, then fill it with warm water and set the thermostat to 90 degrees. All morning, fifteen kids in diapers or swimsuits got in and out of the pool, danced to the "Purple People Eater" song, put their feet up on kid-sized lounge chairs, and drank apple juice from Dixie cups with tiny umbrellas in them. That's what I'm thinking about when I sing the second verse.

Instrumental Bridge

Everything's going along as usual until one afternoon there's a stomach upset that turns into an all-out assault on life as you knew it. In time it morphs into acceptance and transformation. Some might even call it resurrection.

Chorus

Your eyes lit up the sky
set the world on fire

Then repeat the chorus with a new perspective

Two little eyes light up the sky
set the world on fire

When I visit Forrest now, I lie on the ground above him and a little to the right, with a perfect view of the sky.

Set the World on Fire

From somewhere so far away
the wind blew and found its way to me
and then it found you
It circled and spun you 'round
it lifted you off the ground
I knew that you could feel the wind
pull you higher over mountains
to the clouds and through the valley
Your eyes lit up the sky
Set the world on fire

One by one and two by two we loved you
and danced with you
in love with you
You held on you took my hand
you turned me and spun me 'round
'til I was sure to feel the wind
feel the wind
pull me higher over mountains
to the clouds and through the valley
Your eyes lit up the sky
Set the world on fire

*Pull me higher over mountains
to the clouds and through the valley
Your eyes lit up the sky
Set the world on fire*

*Two little eyes light up the sky
Set the world on fire*

*Lie down and be with me forever I'll be with you
and feel the wind*

• Distractions •

Blinded

Peter and I were going through the motions of living together—me making music, keeping house, teaching as often as I could; him going to work every morning, coming home in the afternoon and quickly heading out with binoculars and a camera to look for birds in the woods around our house. There was nothing to complain about but there was no heat running through our veins either. We both needed more than the other could give. Attempts at intimacy were declined with compassion but eventually it turned to hopelessness. I was fifty years old and wondering if I could live without being touched for the rest of my life. Peter felt the same.

A couple of years earlier I had been hired to teach music to kids in New York City who had lost a parent on 9-11. I took an Amtrak train from Rhinecliff Station to 34th Street every Thursday morning to work with them after school.

On one of those Thursdays, I caught the train as usual, found the food car, and sat at a table by a west-facing window so I could watch the Hudson River as we traveled south. It was a typical fall day in the Catskills—chilly with a perfect blue sky, red, orange, and golden yellow leaves on the trees, and the cold dark river moving towards the city. I could watch that river for hours.

When the conductor announced that the breakfast car was open, I got up and stood in line with a few others. The mood was congenial. We didn't know one another, but we talked as though we did.

When I was next in line, waiting, I noticed a man to my left in the last row. He was sitting alone wearing a conductor's uniform.

"Good morning," I said, "you look like you're

headed to work."

He smiled. "Yep. I'll pick-up a train at 34th Street and take it back to Montreal this afternoon."

"You do that every day?"

"A couple of days a week. It's a nice route."

I was just about to tell him I'd lived in White River Junction briefly years before and that I loved hearing the Montrealer scream through town in the middle of the night, but the host at the food counter said, "next," so I said good-bye and wished the conductor well. But I was already snagged. Our conversation had been just what I needed. I felt attractive standing in front of him, a feeling I hadn't had for years.

I bought my tea and took the cardboard box with creamers and headed back to my seat. As I passed the conductor, I said, "have a good trip today." Then I smiled in a way that was both shy and lovely, a trick I'd learned over the years although I'm hardly aware of using it anymore.

Back at my seat, watching the river and sipping my tea, I wondered how much time needed to pass before I could justify a second cup. I knew my motive, but I also knew I needed to appear calm. I decided I'd go back after I finished my first cup, that I would try not to hurry.

"More coffee?" he said as I approached his seat.

"Tea," I said, "I'm not a coffee drinker."

"Me neither."

"Really? I'm surprised."

It was working. I was talking to him and he drank tea!

I stopped and leaned on the back of the chair in front of him.

"My father sells electrical equipment for trains," I said. It was true but probably not that interesting for him to know. "I used to go to bid openings for him at the transit authority when I lived in Brooklyn."

"Is that the place on Livingston Street?"

"Yeah, it is." I said with more enthusiasm than necessary.

The Transit Authority building was where people like my dad bid for orders on insulators, transformers, ball bearings, or anything else the transit authority needed to maintain their network. Bringing it up was the only way I knew of to talk to this man. "I never won a bid, but I learned a lot."

Our conversation went on like that for the rest of

the trip. Eventually I sat down in front of him. We shared insignificant details of our lives that gradually led to more personal stories. I told him about my favorite train ride when I stood on the back deck of a caboose as the train wove through hills and trees from Dunedin to Christchurch in New Zealand. I told him how much I loved watching the landscape move away from me, and that singing "The Long and Winding Road" out there, knowing no one could hear me, had been exhilarating. He told me about his rides from New York to Canada multiple times a week, how he liked the longer routes, seeing the same people over and over again, and how he liked the time he had on the train when he wasn't working. Then he told me about his daughter and his recent divorce. "I'm sorry," I said, even as *available* was floating around my head. I told him about Forrest, and we both got teary. He showed me a picture of his little girl and told me she was the reason he worked as hard as he did. "I'd do anything for her," he said. And I thought about how much I'd like to be her stepmother someday. The loneliness I'd been feeling in my marriage had already led to a list I'd been keeping: *Things I'm looking for if I get another chance: a man with kids and possibly grandchildren / a man who loves his kids and grandchildren / a family who will welcome me and be glad that their father has found me / a family I can spend Thanksgiving with.* My needs were pretty simple, but also desperate. Peter and I were moving away from one another, and Forrest was gone. My future looked empty. I was dissolving into the idea of life with this man I'd just met.

I spent the next week imagining when I would see him again: talking at first, getting to know each other, but then having sex on the train, sex at 34th Street Station, sex wherever we could manage it between Manhattan and Montreal. My dying, drying body was coming back to life. I felt beautiful again, and most of all, I felt like a woman. I'd told myself that being sexless was an aspect of getting older, that it was normal, and that I could live without it. This conductor turned all of that conviction upside down. My imagination was on fire and I liked it.

I talked myself into believing that daydreaming was innocent, so I daydreamed a lot.

When the next Thursday came, I wore my newest underwear, a loose-fitting shirt, and pants with an easy fly. I felt alive and could hardly wait to get to the station.

But my conductor wasn't on the train. I know because I walked the entire length of it as casually as I could, like a person whose legs need stretching.

When I got back to Rhinecliff Station that evening, feeling more distracted than ever, I went to the ticket window.

"Excuse me," I said as I leaned into the glass that separated us. "I'm wondering if you could help me?"

"Sure. Whaddya need?

"Well, it's kind of a strange request. Last week I met a conductor on the morning train to 34th Street. He takes the Montrealer back north in the afternoons? While we were talking, he shared some contact information with me that I've lost." I was making this up, but I needed to find my conductor. "I'm wondering if you might know him and if he'll be on the morning train again?"

He smiled.

And I knew by his smile that he was on to me.

"Hmm. Let's see. I don't know him, but if you leave your card, I'll see what I can do." Then he smiled again as though he might start to laugh.

I left my card, but a different ticket man was at the window when I went back the following Thursday.

I got on the train again, sat in the food car on the west side hoping if I repeated my movements, my conductor would too. Surely the universe would align to make that happen. I convinced myself that it would. When he wasn't on the train, I thought *he must be in the city already. He's gotta pick up his train to Montreal this afternoon.* At 34th Street, I could feel him nearby. *Macy's. He must be at Macy's. He would need lunch, a nice lunch with a good cup of tea. Surely he's at the food court.* So I went there. I crossed 8th Avenue walking with purpose but without getting sweaty. I looked everywhere—in and around the fish, the steaks, the croissants, and the bagels. But he wasn't there so I bought flowers. I had to find him, and when I did, I would give him the flowers and tell him how grateful I was that he brought my body back to life. I would stand at the top of the main stairway at 34th Street Station, and I would wait for over two hours for him to ascend those stairs because I knew he would and I had to thank him. And he would understand. And he wouldn't laugh, he would just say thank you and I would walk away grateful that I had been faithful to Peter and I had been honest with the conductor whose name I still don't remember.

    But he never came.

Blinded by the Love

Please, come on love,
I'm in need, come on love

I don't need a conversation
to know what I'm feeling inside
All I need is that sensation when I see your eyes
And I need your love to bring me around
to heal my heart, to heal my heart

It was just another morning
 like any other autumn day around here
You were near and I was needy
but something was clear
You moved away before we met, never met
Now I'm blinded, blinded by the love

I don't need your lovin'
to know that I heat up just fine
I convinced myself my dreamin'
would make it all right
But I feel!

How do you love? What do you love?

FINDING A WAY

*How do you know if there's something you do
that is good for you or not, good for you or not?*

I'm blinded, so blinded by the love

• Forgiveness •

Breaking Bread

I couldn't sleep that night. Part of it was the 5:00 alarm I'd set for a flight I needed to catch at 9:00 the next morning. Part of it was the icy canyon between me and the airport. It didn't help that the wind was rattling the dryer vent in the next room. But mostly it was because of a story I was trying to write.

I did what I could to calm my busy mind. I counted backwards from ten, I focused on my breath, I even imagined the color blue, a strategy my friend Charlotte swears by. Then I reminded myself that stories and songs write themselves if I leave them alone. They always do. Somehow my mind continues to work on them while I'm asleep. It's a mystery I've learned to count on.

I finally fell asleep around 2:00 having woken up multiple times to scribble solutions to my writing problem on a pad next to my bed. None of them made sense when I read them in the morning.

So on the way to the airport, having navigated the canyon, I started to obsess about my story again. As I drove east, I realized I had the same problem with the story I was writing as I'd had with the song I was trying to write about. Both had beginnings, but I couldn't figure out how to get any further.

I started writing the song in 2009 the night I'd picked up my nylon-string guitar for the first time in years. The day before a musician I'd worked with on a number of projects stopped by to see me. He'd just listened to "Parachute" and the other songs I'd written after Forrest died and wondered if I was interested in hearing what he thought. The question made me nauseous. I've learned to brace myself when someone asks a question like that.

"I don't think you've gone deep enough." He thought my songs were light considering what I'd gone through. "I wanted to feel your grief but what I felt was you trying to make sense of what happened."

His assessment made me angry. But I knew there was some truth in what he was saying. Anger is always a flag of truth.

When I picked up my guitar the next night, I was thinking I'd try to go deeper. I turned down the lights and gave myself permission to sing whatever came out, to cry or wail, or scream if that's what I needed.

All it took was the sound of the guitar.

I'd bought it the week we were in New York City for Forrest's liver resection—the biggest, scariest, and most important surgery of his treatment. If it worked, he might live. If it didn't, he would die. They had to get every bad cell and there were a lot of them. I bought the guitar for 200 bucks at Manny's and played for him at night. It was mid-March and his bed was by the window in the ICU at Columbia Presbyterian Hospital overlooking the East River. The surgeons had put him in a coma so he wouldn't wiggle around. The ventilator tubes were in his lungs. If he moved too much, he could puncture them. He was as still as death.

Hearing that guitar again took me back to my exhaustion and fear, the violent turbulence of the river below me those nights in New York. I played to distract myself then. I needed to connect with the little boy I loved more than the sky, the son I hoped could hear me.

As those nights in the ICU filled my memory I started to weep. Then I started to

sing, and I sang the same line over and over again. *If there's a way to end these tears.*

I wasn't ready to go any further.

I needed to live longer before I could finish.

The story I was trying to write had the same problem: I had a beginning, but I didn't know how to get from there to the larger story I needed to tell. It started with a bread recipe that involved a lot of people I love.

The recipe calls for unbleached flour, whole-wheat flour, brown sugar, Rapid-Rise yeast, warm water, and salt. It came with my marriage to Peter. His sister-in-law Kirsten would make the bread whenever we'd visit, and she baked it for family occasions too.

Smelling her bread in the oven, cutting and

toasting a thick slice, then eating it slathered in butter always reminded me of my surrogate Grandpa in England. Two of his children lived with my father's family during the war and are as much a part of my family as my blood cousins, aunts, and uncles. I used to visit Grandpa regularly. He baked his family's bread recipe every Saturday morning in his cobblestone kitchen by the North Sea. Three loaves would carry him and a guest through the week.

When I visited, we'd cut slices of his bread at teatime and toast them in his fireplace. He was in his 90s then, a widower. After we ate, he'd play the piano while I read and listened. Afterwards, when the sun had gone down, Grandpa would put on his big rubber boots and his old black raincoat and set off for the beach. He liked to walk in silence and never carried a flashlight. When I was there, I'd follow him through the gate and over the dunes, close enough behind that I wouldn't trip or fall. He trusted the stars and the moon for direction, and when there were clouds, he trusted himself.

I was in my mid 20s then and couldn't imagine a more perfect way to live.

When Kirsten gave me her family's bread recipe years later, I tried to replicate Grandpa's life when I baked it. On as many Saturdays as I could, I made three loaves and filled our house with the smell of it. Our loaves didn't last as long. I have a weakness for fresh bread and butter.

When Grandpa taught me how to knead dough, he said it was important to be patient and thorough.

"Work the dough for 30 minutes," he'd say. "Don't be afraid to lean into it."

Like Grandpa, I loved the feel of the dough between my fingers, adding a little flour to take some of the stickiness away.

When I made Kirsten's bread for Peter and me, it felt like I was blending the memory of my English family with my American one, bringing them together to start something new.

I found Kirsten's recipe in the back of a folder I've saved recipes in for years. It was in an envelope along with a note she wrote me when I was a new and welcomed member of the extended family. When I saw it, I knew reading it would be hard. A lot had changed.

The first time I smelled Kirsten's bread Forrest

was three months old. The two of us were visiting Kirsten and her husband Lincoln, Peter's brother. It was our first trip away from home together. He was wearing his light blue fuzzy pajamas balancing on my knee in her living room. I was in the bubble of new motherhood, mesmerized by him, in awe of the miracle of his life and my good fortune. I was as happy as I've ever been in my own skin. But he was gone now. And my marriage with Peter was over too.

People always nod in understanding when they learn we divorced. They've heard that marriages don't survive the death of a child. But it's more complicated than that. Distilling it into one short paragraph is impossible. But the decision to separate was mutual. It wasn't that we had grown apart. We just hadn't grown together in the years after Forrest died. Staying together for whatever years were left seemed like an endurance test we had to pass for other people's benefit rather than a choice that was good for us. We both needed to start over.

Peter decided to stay in the house. I moved to a cottage a few miles away.

Leaving meant more than just separating from

Peter. We'd built that house together. It held everything I had loved and relied on—our family of three, motherhood, the studio we'd built for me to work in, a space I'd dreamed of for years. Saying good-bye meant leaving Peter there to continue on as though I no longer belonged there. The thought makes my heart ache even now. And yet it was time to go, time for me to find a new life that would give me hope again.

Reading Kirsten's recipe was made still harder by the fact that I had fallen in love with Brent, Peter's cousin, and thrown the whole clan into an angry frenzy. When I finally made the bread in the kitchen that Brent and I have built in Colorado, I couldn't help but see the symbolism of kneading the dough, exercising patience, adding another ingredient to make something new, blending yet another layer of my family into one whole that was my life. No writer wants to extend a metaphor, but there it was looking at me in the face.

I met Brent online years after I'd met him briefly at a couple of family occasions. Like everyone in Peter's family, he was reading my blog about Forrest. It was my way of keeping everyone in the loop when he got sick, and then afterwards as I sorted out my grief.

Brent sent an email out of the blue nearly eight years after Forrest died. He wanted to introduce me to a woman he'd recently met. The woman worked in upstate New York and he thought she might be a good connection for me. Brent lived in Baton Rouge. I wrote him back to thank him, and I commented on the work his friend was doing. My email caused him to write me back, then I wrote him, then he wrote me, and before we knew it there was no turning back. I was communicating with the man I'd been imagining for myself for years, the man I'd promised myself I would not turn away from if he ever came into my life.

Everything about loving Brent was right, yet everything about loving Brent was wrong. It threw me into a deep pit of questions I could hardly form let alone answer. Questions about loyalty, family, marriage, love, letting go of love or risking everything to hold onto it. I wrestled endlessly with whether it was right to take care of my needs when it would hurt so many people I loved. The questions wouldn't go away. So I started to take long walks alone in the woods, exhausting myself so I could sleep at night, hoping that sleep would bring answers.

Every day I parked at the bottom of Lewis Hollow Road then started my climb. At the end of the paved road I'd take a right onto a wooded path that led up Overlook Mountain into the Catskills. As I got stronger, I went farther and farther and stayed out longer and longer. There were forks on the path to places I didn't know, and creeks with slippery rocks to cross, but every day I went farther or chose the path I hadn't hiked the day before. When that was no longer a challenge, I left the path. I was testing myself on purpose. I wanted to see how much courage I had, how willing I was to take a risk.

What I found was that I liked it out there.

The plane out of Colorado Springs taxied towards the runway. As it did, I took a quick look around to see who my neighbors were. Over my right shoulder was a young black woman with her six-month-old baby in a snuggly strapped to her chest. He was facing outwards and looking straight at me when I turned around. I smiled. The baby's mother smiled back. Her smile welcomed me into her orbit, which was what I was hoping for.

"Good morning," I said, looking at her wide-eyed son. "What a beauty you are."

He stared at me, trying to focus.

"Is this your first time?" I asked.

"It is," his mother said.

And just like that my eyes were spilling over. Silent tears I had to hide from the mother I'd just met. The memory of my first flight with Forrest flooding back into me: Philadelphia to San Francisco, seven days before Forrest's cancer slammed into me—the two of us, Forrest and me, sitting in the very last row on a single seat that couldn't recline. Me carrying way too much baby paraphernalia to manage alone, him full of tumors attached to his liver, stomach, heart, and lungs—tumors I didn't know about yet. I couldn't help but wonder what hardships the little boy behind me would face in his lifetime, not the least of which was the color of his perfect light brown skin.

Within seconds of tears streaming down my face, I was a writer again, trying to put into words what I was feeling. Detaching myself from the hurt and moving into observer mode. Thinking to myself *this is perfect. I'm trying to write a story about tears and here they are for me to look at.* I let them fall for as long as I could.

To compose myself I finally turned on my kindle.

On a whim, I clicked on a book I'd started weeks before written by Jimmy Webb, the songwriter who wrote "Witchita Lineman," "Up, Up, and Away," and "The Moon is a Harsh Mistress." His book is called *Tunesmith* and gets into pretty specific detail about how a good song is put together. The page I opened to was about rhyme.

Without using my name, Webb condemned the song I'm trying to tell you about. He says songs without a strong rhyme scheme are amateurish (mine hardly has one). Not only that, the metaphor I used in my first verse describing tears as something related to the ocean, is a no-no (don't do it, he says, it's been done already and doesn't need to be done again). Worst of all, he says maudlin songs are of no use. All of this is my memory of what I read. Surely it wasn't as black and white as all that.

I sat on the plane restraining my tears again, thinking about how much I love the song I eventually called "If There's a Way." In fact, when someone asks me who my favorite songwriter is, I think to myself *me*, because it's true even if I answer Lennon and McCartney.

If my songs weren't my favorite how could I keep writing them?

But as the plane climbed into the clouds I thought, *who wants to read a story about a crooked, unrhyming song they've probably never heard before? Who cares?*

And my answer was *me* again. I care. I think about it all the time: how my songs came into being, how I want to tell you how they happened and what happened to me or within me to cause them into existence. I want you to know that the words *I would lie down before an altar of stone/And watch a songbird flying over the hill* are literal. I'd lay on the ground next to Forrest's grave for long periods of time, daydreaming, talking to him, looking up at the sky, watching the birds and wondering if my days as a singer were over. And that what I learned from this song is that everything I've done since the first night I sang *if there's a way to end these tears*, turned out to be the way.

If There's a Way

If there's a way to end these tears
so they won't fall forever after or years
or overflow drowning all of my dreams
I'd catch them all,
give them back to the sea to find a way

At dawn I would lie down before an altar of stone
watch a songbird flying over the hill
I would wander high above the tree line
to see a full moon rise
I'd linger 'til the morning light to find a way

I would give up everything I know
I would learn to love again
I would empty every pocket I own
I would carry the hardest sticks and stones
to find a way

I would try to build a shelter without a border or walls
where I would sit by a bridge
and I would listen to the water fall

• L o v e •

Valentine

On Valentine's Day a year and five days after Forrest died, I was desperate to get a message to him, so I shuffled around in the snow until there was a ten-foot heart on our front yard. When I was finished, I drove into town to buy as many red roses as I could. I pulled them all from their stems and scattered the petals all over my frozen valentine. It was beautiful, all that red on perfect snow. I felt better having done something and figured if Forrest *could* see it, he *would* see it.

Around that time, a piano melody was finding its way to my fingers. It sounded like a 21st century version of "Streets of Laredo." I couldn't shake the image of a cowboy entering my song on a horse. I couldn't understand why he was there and what I should do about him, so I ignored him and wrote about a bluebird instead.

Seventeen years later, I still see that cowboy when I play the song I eventually called "Valentine." He rides into my mind on a velvet-black horse with his sweaty gray hat, a holster, and muddy leather spats. But I also see my bluebird. She's a watercolor animation in my mind, flitting from here to there, arriving at a tree where she sings to Forrest who's somewhere I can't get to. I like seeing them all, but I wish the music aligned better with the bluebird.

My rose petal valentine disappeared within a few hours. When I looked out the window that afternoon to check on it, the only thing left was a single set of deer tracks heading into the woods. That deer had eaten my valentine. I laughed and cried at the same time. My friend Kirsti calls that happysad.

Valentine

On Valentine's
I'll send my love through the bluebird
I will sing for her
then she will sing for you
fly through the sky to heaven above

She will know you, Love, sing her song to remind you
She will find a way to tell you how much I love you

And when the day is over
I'll hear her little melody
dream it as I fall asleep

I love you
Three little words that mean so much
Three little words are all I need
when it's time to say goodbye

• Trust •

A Little Love

Brent and I were finally in the same room. Months of emails and the occasional hand-written note had brought us closer than I'd ever been with a man. Words and longing were holding us together. I'd written him a song the month before and imagined him reaching out to hold me with tears and gratitude in his eyes when I played it for him. I recorded it not knowing if I would have the courage to sing it for him live.

There was a bed in the darkened room where we stood looking at one another, not exactly sure where to go from there.

I couldn't wait. "Could we lie down for a minute?"

"Why?" he asked, as though I were moving too fast.

"Just give me a minute. I have a something for you"

He put his head on the pillow as I fumbled with my Walkman and the ear buds that were in a knot from traveling. When he was settled, I sat down next to him, put the buds in his ears and pressed play. I could hear my song bleeding from the headphones as I put my head on his chest.

Almost immediately his eyes popped open and he started to fidget.

"I can't hear it. We need to turn it up."

His fingers were too big to spin the volume control. He was distracted and annoyed with himself. We were both frustrated as the song kept playing and the romance of hearing it together disappeared. Eventually we got the volume right, so I re-started the song. Brent reached for me just as I'd hoped he would, but it wasn't the moment I'd imagined. We didn't cry together or have a long satisfying kiss. Instead, we learned a little more about one another: Brent is nearly deaf in one ear.

I'm a dreamer who is easily disappointed.

Later we lay in bed, tired, content, and a little confused by our awkward lovemaking. It had been a long time for both of us and we weren't kids anymore. No flat belly for him, and no youthful thighs for me; 8000 feet of altitude making every effort more difficult. We kept the lights low to protect ourselves from reality. Eventually he got up to get some food. He came back with a plate full of 2-inch squares of cheddar cheese. Our first meal together. No crackers or bread. Just cheese. It was too soon to tease him, but I wanted to.

Then he disappeared again, this time for a bottle of wine. When he came back, we sat on the bed and drank from plastic cups. There wasn't much to say. We'd already shared what we needed to say in letters back and forth: excitement, fear, anticipation, uncertainty, and a certainty that outweighed any questions we still had. He kept touching my fingers as though he couldn't believe I was there. I watched him touch me, hoping it would never end. Eventually we lay down to sleep. He was on his back; I lay on my belly with my arm across his chest. Within moments he was purring his now familiar purr. I listened as I relaxed into the closeness of him. It was as peaceful as I'd felt in years.

Without thinking, I began to hum like I did as a kid when I was hungry and my mother's cooking hit the spot. Then I started to sing the song I'd written for Brent. *Here I am again/I'm in love with you.* It was a whisper. I didn't know if he could hear me, but I could hear myself. It was the quietest sound I'd ever made. It felt pure and true. I didn't need for Brent to hear me. What I needed was to love someone enough to sing for them without hesitation. My song was a lullaby for both of us. When I was done, he pulled me into his chest and wept.

A Little Love Can Mean A Lot

Here I am again
I'm in love with you
You're the man I want
but I can't get next to you
when you're not here

I have imagined you
I have dreamed of you
I have asked for a time when a man like you
would come for me
and here you are

Sometimes a little love can mean a lot
In time a little love can mean a lot

You respond to me
You reach out for me
You hear my words
then I hear your words and they comfort me
when you're not here

Sometimes a little love can mean a lot
With time a little love could mean a lot
It means a lot

Here I am again
I'm in love with you
You're the man I love but I can't get enough of you
when you're not here

I have imagined you
I have dreamed about you too
I have prayed for a time
when you would come and rest with me
and here you are
Here we are!

Sometimes a little love can mean a lot
This time a little love will mean a lot

• Mystery •

A Conversation

In the days and weeks after Forrest died, I sat for hours in front of the bay window in our living room staring into the sky, imagining Forrest looking back at me. I cried a lot, I talked to him a lot, I tried to make sense of his physical absence. I imagined him moving further and further away from me. It felt like he'd merged with the sky in the same way smoke or steam would. I told myself all I had to do was breathe to bring him closer. When I was willing, the sky was visible proof of God. Other times it was just sky. Some days I'd talk to God just in case there were ears out there listening. Then I sang to God.

By the time I sang what became the final verse of my new song, it was as though God and I were old friends. All I had to do was sing if I wanted to be in touch.

I can't prove this because the tape I was recording on that day has disappeared, but the moment I finished singing my song to God all the way through for the first time, the front door of our house blew open on an otherwise calm summer day.

Oh God

Oh God, can I ask you this?
Oh God, can you tell me this?
Can you hear me when I sing?

Oh God, tell me where he is
Oh God, please tell me where he is
I can't hear you, can't you sing, Oh God?

Oh God, I can tell you this
Oh God, I sure want to tell you this
I can hear you when I sing, Oh God

• Friendship •

Filled up

It was time to call my friend Abby again. I often call her when I'm frustrated with a new song or a story I'm trying to write. As soon as I say, "I'm stuck," she says, "So write about that." It's good advice. When I got off the phone, I wrote *I have no idea what I want to say in this song. I don't have a first line to work from, I don't have a chorus to work towards, and I have no clue what I want to say by the end. But I like the music. It makes me happy. Besides, I need to write a fun song. My songs are too serious. I don't know how to write a fun song. I need to know how to write a fun song.*

But writing all of that didn't help. I still didn't have a clue and I wasn't enjoying myself either.

Long before I called Abby that day, I had sent my

recorded piano track to Peter Tomlinson, a good friend who's also a pianist. I half expected him to say *give it up, Bar, it's not happening*. Instead, he pulled a snare drum out of his closet and played a non-stop rolling beat with my song that sounded like a train coming down the tracks. Then he added a twangy steel guitar. The song was turning into something, but I still didn't know what that was.

A few months later, Lou Pappas rehearsed the song with us and played an oompah part on his upright bass: 5-1-5-1-5-1-5-1, back and forth like a tuba player. I didn't like it. It sounded like a polka and I don't always like polkas. I said, "nah, it's too corny, Lou. Can you play something less busy?" I hope I was nice about it. But when he did, the song went flat again. He was right the first time. His original part had energy and motion; the song was finally going from somewhere to somewhere else. We recorded Peter and Lou's parts for a new album the next day. My call for help to Abby happened a year later. Lyrics had proven elusive. Everything I tried to write was cliché or boring. I was thinking too much. Not having fun. The only line I had but didn't know what to do with was *without a rearview mirror*. I didn't know why it was there or how it fit but I kept going back to it. I liked the way it sounded more than anything else.

After months of trying different lyrics and writing page after page of ideas that still weren't working, I decided to post the music we'd recorded on Facebook. I asked my friends to share anything that came to mind while they were listening to the track. Within a few hours I had a list: my sister Cackie said it sounded like kids on swings and seesaws at a playground. My friend Marcy said it made her think of Thelma and Louise and the Thunderbird she'd always dreamt of owning. Amy the librarian said it felt like riding her bike without a helmet down a steep hill. Like me, a lot of people said it sounded like a train speeding down the tracks.

My favorite response came a week later via snail mail from my Aunt Mary McElroy. She'd grabbed a pen and a small white napkin just before she'd pressed play to hear the song. Her letter said that during a music history course in college, she'd learned to draw while she was listening to Bach, Mozart and Debussy. During exams she could remember her drawings, which helped her remember who she'd been listening to while she drew. Her strategy gave her what she needed to pass the course. She used the same technique with my song. Her napkin had rows and rows of squiggles on it. They looked like endless mountains, or the zigzag pattern on a sewing machine. Below the squiggles on the front side were two parallel lines, wavy like a river. In the top right corner, she'd drawn the sun like a child would draw one. Aunt Mary was having fun and I loved that. Her drawing inspired the second verse:

> *Mary M drew zigs and zaggles*
> *like a million mountains*
> *and a river round the bend*

Someone wrote that the music sounded like a herd of steer or horses running close and fast across the plains. That made me think of my friend Elin who's a cowgirl. I took photographs of her rounding up a dozen horses during a photography workshop Brent and I hosted on her ranch in Colorado.

My mother's college roommate said it sounded

like a carousel. In her mind, there were lovers kissing one another as they went around and around on colorful wooden horses. Another friend said it sounded like snow. And still another said it reminded her of how she feels when her day's unraveling.

Now when I hear the song or I sing it, all of my Facebook friends who responded come to mind. It's one of the great dividends of sharing the process with them. When I invited them in, I started to enjoy myself.

Now, years after finishing the lyrics, the meaning of the line *without a rearview mirror* seems so obvious. I had just left everything I loved behind: my marriage, my home, my friends, my family, my professional life on the east coast. I'd gotten to a crossroads. I didn't want to be known as the mom who'd lost her son anymore. I didn't want to be the wife who was lonely all the time. I didn't want to continue performing the same songs to the same people in the same venues for the rest of my life. I was grateful for all of it, but I had gotten bored with myself. Everything had gotten stale.

When I met Brent, I allowed myself to change my

storyline. With that change came plenty of guilt for the upset I'd caused so many people I'd loved. The line *without a rearview mirror* was my heart telling me to move on, to enjoy my new life, to stop beating myself up.

Roll Over Me

Don't know how to start it
Don't know how to end
Don't know where the bridge is
somewhere up ahead

Mary M drew zigs and zaggles
like a million mountains and a river 'round the bend
Roll over me
Fill me up with things I'd never see and I'll sing

They say it sounds like a train that's travelin'
or a day unravelin' or a kid that's on a swing
Snow fallin', see-sawin'
ridin' your bike in the wind without a rearview mirror

Kisses and carousels
Drivin' a Thunderbird
Gallopin' with a big herd without a rearview mirror
Roll over me
Fill me up with things I'd never see and I'll see

• Ownership •

A Good Long Drink

It was late on a summer night in Woodstock. I was playing my guitar. A breeze was coming through the open windows in my studio. Peter was already in bed. We often went to bed at different times. He was tired after a day of work, and I was avoiding the loneliness I felt when we lay next to each other.

Within a few minutes I was playing a pattern I liked and started to hum along. I'm not a great player so I tend to play one or two simple chords back and forth until I feel comfortable with them. My weakness as a player is often what makes the beginning of a song. It takes me so long to get chords to move smoothly from one to the other that by the time they do, I've started hearing a melody. Once that melody has grown on me, I'm reluctant to change it by adding more chords, so I don't.

On that night humming with those first two chords, I sang *I was born in a wishing well*. But that's as far as I got.

Within a year, Peter and I were divorced. Eighteen months later, I left Woodstock for good. My life with Brent was about to begin in rural Colorado. The day I got in my car to drive west from Woodstock was a lonely one. I'd been in upstate New York for nearly twenty years. Forrest was buried in the ground. His life and death had been headline news in our local paper. On top of that, I'd been singing in the area for twenty years. I was leaving my friends, my neighbors, my fans, and all the people who had kept me whole while Forrest was alive and after he died. Woodstock was home. Leaving without some sort of gathering felt wrong, but it was the only way I could do it. I'd said good-bye to my closest friends the night before. Saying good-bye to the entire community was impossible.

As I drove east on Route 28 to get on the New

York State Thruway, I wrote down the names of every person I could think of in Woodstock so I wouldn't forget them. I wrote until I couldn't think of anyone else. The list was long. As I added names the list began to have a rhythm. Some of the names were filled in with details. Brian, the mailman who always said hi to me, was coupled with Hillary Clinton. The three of us share a birthday. Pam was linked to vegan food. Peter to Amy, the woman he would eventually marry. Another Pam to Gypsy Wolf. Abby to writing, and Dawn to the animals she sat with as they died on the side of the road, cars taking their lives, she not willing to let them die alone. There were so many names, all of them linked to a life I was moving away from. A life I loved. Driving away I felt like I was leaving under the cover of darkness, as though I had let an entire community down by not telling them I was going away. For years, everyone in town knew my business. I'd broadcast it widely when Forrest got sick. I'd blogged, I'd written a book, I'd trusted everyone with my heart, and they had taken good care of it. But I was confused about what was right and what was wrong about loving Brent. I couldn't tell anyone what was happening or why it was time for me to go. Our partnership began too close on the heels of long marriages. I didn't want to know who thought it was courageous and who thought it was shameful. It was all too dear to me to be impacted by other people's judgments. Despite twenty years of being cared for and applauded, both for my music and my mothering, I needed to leave without a word.

Westcliffe, Colorado where Brent and I started our life together, is at 8000 feet in the Wet Mountain Valley east of the Sangre de Cristo Mountains, population 650 in winter, maybe a thousand in summer. I felt relief as soon as I got there. I wasn't the grieving mother anymore. I wasn't the singer-songwriter trying to succeed or compete. I wasn't Peter's wife, and I wasn't Forrest's mom. I didn't have to pass Supertots on the way to the grocery store, and I wouldn't run into Forrest's friends or their parents anymore. As much as I loved all of those things, in Colorado I was anonymous and all of that ended. It was good for me at first.

Over time, though, I began to struggle. With

distance, I could see how much I'd relied on the love I was so freely given back in New York. I hadn't realized how much I needed applause either until there wasn't any. My ego was taking a hit. I didn't know what to do with myself. I wondered if I still wanted to make music, or if I really was a musician at all. For over thirty years, I had sung wherever I could—in the shower, in my car, washing dishes, walking the dogs, concerts within driving distance nearly every week. When I got to Colorado, I didn't sing at all. Had I been doing concerts all those years just to get attention? That was hard to believe, but why had I stopped?

Then every so often I'd sing in the bathroom where the acoustics are so good and I'd remember what I loved about hearing my voice: experimenting with timbres, playing around with rhythms, digging into the richness of the lowest parts of my range. Singing without inhibition. When I'd sing like that, I wouldn't even feel guilty loving the sounds I made. It was like admiring someone else's voice, wishing they could hear her too. But the people who knew my voice were 1600 miles away.

*

Jeffrey Brown did an interview on the *Newshour* with the violinist Joshua Bell. Bell talked about the difference between performing unannounced in a Washington D.C. train station where few people stopped to listen, versus playing at the same station months later when his performance had been advertised. A lot more people stopped when they knew it was Bell playing. He went on to describe how he needed to be heard, how he needed the attention. Then he talked about how the music itself needed to be heard; that it wasn't about him. I knew what he meant. Having an audience is a critical piece for most musicians. We want you to listen. We want you to understand. We want you to care about the music we're playing. That's what I was missing in my life.

Two years after I'd been in Colorado, I called Abby again. I needed help with the song I'd started back in Woodstock while Peter was asleep.

"I have the first line," I told her, "*I was born in a wishing well*, but that's all I've got."

I knew I wanted to write about the dreams I'd had for myself, but that's all I could tell her.

"I don't like the idea of your being in a well," she said. "It scares me. How 'bout next to the well? Or beside the well?"

It was just the question I needed.

Imagining myself *in* a well was scary for me too. All I could think was *no one can hear me. They'll never find me down here.* The idea made me sweat. I suppose I could have written about that, but that wasn't what I wanted to write about. When I imagined myself outside the well, everything changed. I could see myself being seduced by the well, wanting to go near it, curious about it, looking down into it, throwing pennies into it, and finally leaning over and singing into it. There was action and my imagination was animated.

I settled on *near the well* because the word 'near' gave me space and a choice about whether to go closer or farther away from the well.

Changing that one word from 'in' to 'near' created a whole new picture in my head. As soon as it changed, I remembered the only well I'd ever cared about. It was at the bottom of a hill next door to my grandparents' house in Bryn Mawr. We used to sled there in the winter. Afterwards, she'd have hot chocolate by the fireplace. That well, that hill, and that living room represented everything good about my childhood. But when I was a kid, I understood that the well at the bottom of the hill was off limits, hazardous. It was hidden under fallen branches. The stone building around it had been painted white many years before. The paint was mostly gone, and the roof was deteriorating, but because I was told to stay away, I wanted to go in.

In my song, the well became a metaphor for my dreams. I thought about all the coins I'd thrown into wells and pools in my lifetime. Wanting something—money, love, a record contract—but more than anything, I'd wanted to sing. I'd wanted to sing for the whole world. Not for fame, I thought, but because my voice was a gift I was meant to give back. It felt like my destiny. And yet, by the time I was writing the lyrics to my new song, I was mostly unknown despite years of singing in public. I wondered what that said about my voice. Wasn't it good enough? Had I misunderstood my purpose? Shouldn't the gift of my voice have translated into more success?

As I thought about all of these things, my song

began to take shape. I could see myself looking into the well as a young woman, dreaming about what could be. I could hear myself and it was beautiful—full of reverb, depth, and a rich darkness. All I wanted was for someone else to hear me, and that thought made my dreams grow bolder and larger. I began to think about concert halls, band mates, costumes, and award ceremonies. All of these were dreams I told no one about. Thinking like that was quietly discouraged when I was growing up. Better to avoid drawing attention to one's self.

Writing the lyrics reminded me how real my dreams had been:

> *Looked down in to the wishing well*
> *wished I may when I heard myself.*
>
> Wish I may, wish I might,
> have the wish I wish tonight.

I'd never shared my dreams with the people who loved me most. I didn't tell my parents. I didn't tell my siblings or my friends, and I didn't tell myself. I didn't want to be prideful or appear overly ambitious. Instead, I told myself if I was good enough, I'd be discovered. I'd like to say I know better now, but I don't. I still feel like if I keep singing someone will hear me. But who that someone is, is a mystery. Why are one person's ears more important than another's? My dream had been for the powerful one to hear me; the one who could make it possible for a million others to hear me. Had I articulated this to myself when I was twenty might I have had a different outcome? If I said it out loud even now would it make a difference?

There are lines in my writing that I like better than others. Usually I like them because they tell me something about myself I didn't know before. The lyric in the bridge of my new song is one of those lines. As I imagined my well, I saw myself going back there over and over again.

> *One hundred thirty-one buckets of water*
> *drawn from that well*
> *Each sip I took made me thirstier*
> *for more and more of myself*

I was like Narcissus at the pool, but I was also like any artist who loves what they've created: I wanted more of it and I wanted to know more about myself.

While I was writing the tag at the end of the song, I learned one more thing about myself that surprised me. It was an accident like it so often is in songwriting. I was recording as I sang randomly to see if the right words would come out. I started with the first line again: *I was born near a wishing well.* Then I unconsciously added *far away from here.* For the next two lines I thought I'd sung *it feels so far away when I turn to look.* But when I listened back to what I'd recorded I heard this instead:

It's not so far away when I turn to look

I thought I'd been singing about physical distance, and about the dreams I once had. Instead I was discovering that my dreams were still very much alive.

Admitting to myself that my dreams hadn't gone away allowed me to make sense of the nonsense lyrics I'd been singing over the chorus until then, and which I thought I'd eventually throw out:

I sing ah ha ha, mmm, hey, hey, hey

I'd sung those words unconsciously at first. Now I could see I was making light of my narcissism while feeling affection for my younger self too.

While I was making sense of the song, the song was making sense of me.

Ah ha ha

*I was born near a wishing well
overgrown when a red oak fell
hidden in the view
no one else ever knew*

*Looked down into the wishing well
Wished I may when I heard myself
Fell under its spell
All my wishes held
      I sing ah ha ha, mmm, hey, hey, hey*

*Someone said, "you can never tell.
Won't come true, you could go to hell!"
Don't know what to do if I can't tell you
      I Sing ah ha ha, mmm, hey, hey, hey*

*One hundred thirty-one buckets
of water drawn from that well
Each sip I took made me thirstier
for more and more of myself*

*I was born near a wishing well
far away from here
Ah, it seems so far away when I turn, if I turn to look*

BAR SCOTT

Ah, it's not so far away when I turn, if I turn and look
I sing ah ha ha, hmm,
When I turn, when I look, I sing ah ha ha
When I turn, when I drink, I sing ah ha ha
When I turn and I drink, I sing, Ahhh

• P a t i e n c e •

This Lane is My Lane

During a visit home last year, I drove down Rose Glen Road to see what had become of the building where Kajem Recording used to be. There had been so much rain in Philadelphia that spring that the canopy overhead felt heavy and a little claustrophobic. As I got closer to the building, I could feel the excitement of my first visit again. But when I pulled up, there were warning signs posted on the locked gates, the windows were covered with plywood, and the concrete loading dock was crumbling on all sides. The rusted hoist above it dangled even more precariously than it had forty years earlier, and the plastic siding on the stairway was torn and covered with mold.

I wondered if the walls that enclosed the studio inside were still standing; if the tight-fitting doors had kept the interior space from melting away. Walking into Kajem that first time had been the beginning of a dream I didn't know how to dream yet. It's a memory so vivid it's hard to believe forty years have gone by.

For years after Joe and his partners closed the studio, I drove down to that deserted mill and walked along the creek as often as I could. I dreamed of buying the place, reviving it, living inside, making my own music there. During that time, I recorded endlessly on my four-track cassette recorder. One of the patterns I played over and over again stayed with me for thirty-two more years. When I finally got around to writing the lyrics in 2013, it made sense to describe some of what had happened in the interim.

There had been songs and stories, husbands and friends, money earned, and a lot more spent. There was Forrest, and Peter, and choices to make. There were masks and costumes, concerts and commissions. New York and Woodstock, Philadelphia and Colorado. I'd felt pleasure and boredom, insecurity and confidence. At moments I was ambitious, but mostly I was ambiguous. I'd bought gear like a junkie: keyboards, computers, guitars, timbales, anything, I told myself, that would make me a better musician, anything that would keep the thrill alive.

All of it was the stuff of my life.

And through it all, that musical pattern had stayed with me. It was a mystery. But any melody that stayed with me that long deserved to have lyrics. When I started to write them, they unfolded like a poem. They made sense and no sense at the same time, but I liked the way the words sounded as they came out of my mouth.

When I couldn't find the one word that would allow me to finish the song—a pattern I'm just seeing now—I posted my problem on Facebook: *I need a 3-syllable word that ends in 'y' to name a road or a lane someone might turn onto. Any ideas?*

Within the hour, over a hundred people had written back. Their suggestions included reverie, loverly, melody, harmony, majesty, poetry, verity, mystery, workaday, and hoppity. It was fun to think about how each of their words would change the song. *Harmony* could work but for some reason it made me think of Julie Andrews singing *the hills are alive* in the Alps, which was not the image I was looking for. *Reverie* appealed to me but was hard to sing with all those Rs. I liked *melody*, but I'd already used it in the first verse. In the end, *poetry* made the most sense. It was easy enough to sing even if Ps pop and peak when they're sung in front of a microphone. With practice, I could turn my mouth away from the mic at just the right moment to soften the P. Then I made it harder on myself by having three Ps in the chorus.

> *Look how pennies are won!*
> *Pick a road and run*
> *Turn down Poetry Lane or tango with someone*

In 2016 I won a plastic cutting board from the New School's Creative Writing Department for my 6-word memoir. It said *Everything I've done is behind me.* That's what this song is about, and I'm grateful for all of it.

Journey

Look how the world turned out
with all its colors and finery
song melodies
lovers and linings
mothers and rhyming

Friends cycle, faux lashes,
your eyes, and my passion

Journey, you're an angel,
a wave, a clock in time
You're a word and a line

Look how pennies are won!
Pick a road and run
Turn down Poetry Lane or tango with someone

A new heart beating,
A garden, a seedling,
a baby

Journey, you're an angel
a wave, a clock in time,

you're a word or a line
you're a meadow in the morning,
    a heron in the sky
    you're a cloud and a kite

    harmony, melody, symphony, parody,
you're a homily, unity, fantasy, eulogy,
you're a holiday, reverie, family, energy
you're a mystery to me
you're a walk in the park

Look how it all turned out
with all its colors and memory

Look how it all turned out!

Gratitude

Doris Dembosky for picking up the phone
Nicole Parsons for midrash and a seriousness I recognize
Donna Miller for responding
Tim Cumerford for willingness
Arthur Katsapis for believing
Kevin Robinson for getting it
Holly Tripp for honesty and smarts
Jenny Redfield Costner for love and protection
Dorothy Allison for permission
Abigail Thomas for regular reminders
Brent Bruser, my sweet man, for the big things
safe-haven, time, space, home
Lucy Swenson for forever love
Erin Papa for years of taking care of me
Leah Hanes for clarity
Annie Scholl Hampton for the search
Dawn Casteel-Lorrick for being you
Jacqueline Whitmore for sharing
Charlene and Jim Andres-Rohr for cheerleading
Martha Frankel for inclusion
Kitty Sheehan for your message. I've kept it with my
manuscript since the day you sent it
Ted Orland and David Bayles for your book *Art and Fear*
Amy Schindler and Maire Tashjian for constancy
Stacey Haber for tenacity
Ann Staley for poetry
Chuck Elliot for airplay
Lorraine Salmon for home away from home, fizzy drinks,
and fearlessness in the face of Mr. Rat

Kirsti Gholson for harmony
Chris Kerr for loving me too
Steve Dagirmanjian for kindness
Peter Tomlinson for jumping all the way in.
There has been no one else like you
Lou Pappas for the groove and a guest room
Dave Cook for your ears and heart
Jen Starr, Erica Cohn and Callie Hershey
for years of singing together
Mare Wakefield for healing
My parents, Mary and Buck Scott
for their consistent and reliable goodness
My siblings—Mary Scott, Sally Moser, Cackie Scott,
Caroline McIlhenney, and Bill Scott—for foundation
Cackie Scott and Brian Vesley for hotel services
Mary McElroy for that napkin and the story behind it
Lee and Peter Scott for saving me
Bobby Conway for a couch when I needed to rest
and the boot when I needed to move along
Sarah Conway, you might not have known
how much I needed you
My Facebook friends for playing along
Roger Bach and Rita DeNoble for teaching me so much
To the writers who have trusted me with your pages,
did you know you were saving me?
To Melodie Kauff for a critical question about my beliefs.
If I were to sum it up, I'd say we're here to create, and from
what we create, we are created.
And Forrest, for being the most important creative act of my life. I love you more than the sky. No matter where you go, no matter what you do, I will always love you.

"Good Long Drink" first appeared as "Ah ha ha" in
Corners: Voices on Change, Jack Walker Press, 2018

"Breaking Bread" first appeared in
The Bacopa Literary Review, 2017

"The Ways of Water" first appeared on
Raven's Perch online magazine, 2017

"Before and After" first appeared as "Heaven" in
Stories of Music, Volume Two, Timbre Press, 2016

"Simple Gifts" first appeared as "Grace"
in *Stories of Music, Volume One,* Timbre Press, 2014

A version of "Valentine" first appeared in
Three Minus One, SheWrites Press, 2011

About the Author

Bar Scott has been making music and writing songs for nearly forty years. Her albums include *Journey, Parachute, Grapes and Seeds, Confession, and Silence is Broken*. Her books include *The Present Giver*, and *The Lone Writer's Writing Club – a Workbook for Writers Who Wish They Had a Writing Group*. She takes photographs and makes collage on in-between days, and she works with other writers and musicians to help them do more of what they love to do. You can find her at barscott.com. An audio version of this book narrated by Bar is available wherever you get your audio books.